New Jersey Retirement Roadmap

A Definitive Guide to Successfully Retiring
and Thriving in the Garden State

William Skillender

William Skillender Wealth Management
BRIELLE, NEW JERSEY

William Skillender/William Skillender Wealth Management
101 Union Ave., Brielle, NJ 08730
williamskillender.com

Ordering Information:
Quantity sales. Special discounts are available on quantity purchases by corporations, associations, and others. For details, contact the "Special Sales Department" at the address above.

New Jersey Retirement Roadmap/William Skillender — 1st ed.
ISBN 9798858549918

Contents

SECURITIES AND ADVISORY DISCLOSURES

Securities and advisory services offered through Madison Avenue Securities, LLC (MAS), member of FINRA/SIPC, and a registered investment advisor. MAS and William Skillender Wealth Management Tax Advisory are not affiliated entities.

Investing involves risk, including the potential loss of principal. It is not possible to invest in an index. Any references to protection, safety, or lifetime income generally refer to fixed insurance products, never securities or investments. Insurance guarantees are backed by the financial strength and claims-paying abilities of the issuing carrier.

This book is intended for informational purposes only. It is not intended to be used as the sole basis for financial decisions, nor should it be construed as advice designed to meet the particular needs of an individual's situation.

Our firm is not permitted to offer and no statement made during this presentation shall constitute tax or legal advice. Our firm is not affiliated with or endorsed by the U.S. Government or any governmental agency.

The information and opinions contained herein provided by third parties have been obtained from sources believed to be reliable, but accuracy and completeness cannot be guaranteed by our firm.

Dedicated to my Aunt Marilyn . . . who has worked tirelessly in my office to help our clients.

And who represents all of my family, friends, and clients whom God has already called home (too soon in many cases). Someday, a long time from now, I may retire (or at least slow down) but Aunt Marilyn will still be here giving the clients the love and attention that makes a difference.

Finding My Purpose

In the mid-1970s when I was attending G. Harold Antrim Elementary School in Point Pleasant Beach, New Jersey, I was tested in math. My third-grade teacher, Ms. Iorio, had suspected that I might be cheating on my tests. So, they took me aside and put me under watchful eyes to see how I was able to score perfect (or almost perfect) in the advanced math exams that they administered. I was actually brought into the principal's office. He was loved and adored by everyone, and the idea of doing anything to disappoint him was devastating to my young mind. Mr. Palisi looked at me sternly and said something to the effect of, "Billy, I can't believe you would cheat on your exam. You're better than this." He made me feel terrible. I was left doubting myself and wondering if I really *was* cheating.

However, after being observed under a fully secure monitoring system (1970s version), it was discovered and concluded that not only was I not cheating, but I had an exceptional gift for math and numbers that went well beyond my age. I was both relieved and nervous; I wasn't used to excelling in anything and honestly considered almost everyone else around me to be much smarter.

As I got older, it was suggested that I go on a fast track for engineering or some other mathematics-intensive career. But those things bored me. I'd much rather do something that was "people-oriented" and not be stuck behind a desk with numbers growing out of my head. In fact, the idea of that kind of career made me sad; I thought it was just a terrible irony that the very thing I excelled at was something I found boring and uninteresting.

Fortunately, through a very winding road, my life's work and mission were found in investment advising and financial planning—specifically for retirees in Monmouth and Ocean Counties in New Jersey. Nothing is more fulfilling to me than being able to take the world of the stock market and investments and put it all in a specific plan that is personalized and unique to each of my individual clients and their families. I've learned—and continue to learn—that the people in our lives are the most important. Our assets, income, investments, etc., are supposed to be the tools that help us live our lives in the best way that each of us is meant to.

For those of us who've lived here all our lives, we know that the Jersey Shore (not the TV show) is a special place with so much to offer. It is my hope that if you're fortunate enough to live and even retire here, this roadmap can help you make the most of your golden years. And if you're ever near either of my offices in Brielle or Rumson, please stop in to say hello and let me know if this book has helped you at all.

CHAPTER 1

Falling into Place—or Falling Apart?

There are certain times in life when it feels like everything is falling into place. It's like nothing can go wrong. I always loved the phrase, "the world is your oyster." It represented what a lot of us felt in the 1990s in Central Jersey and even in most of the United States: we had it good.

At least, that was our perception.

The start of the new millennium was such a time for me. As 2000 arrived, I was in my early thirties, and things could not have been better. I was in a great relationship with a wonderful girl. I had an awesome group of friends and family that loved me and had my back. I was working in my dream career as an options trader at a private equity firm out of Philadelphia and doing so well financially that I envisioned opening up my own firm. I pictured myself retiring in five to ten years and touring the country as a celebrity financial wizard, giving lectures and signing autographs.

I had learned much in the '90s about myself and about life. Growing up "down the Jersey Shore" seemed to offer a unique perspective on everything. My small-town roots from Point Pleasant Beach, New Jersey, seemed to be a great foundation for what I perceived to be everything that loomed ahead. I really thought I had it all figured out. Little did I realize, I had nothing figured out.

Life has a way of punching you in the gut just when you think nothing could go wrong.

Trading equities and options in the '90s made me believe I was brilliant. I would follow some simple chart patterns that basically said that if Yahoo or Amazon goes down, don't worry. Just hold onto it, and it will go back up. Brilliant, right? Well, it actually worked—that is, until what became known as the Dot-com bubble started to burst in 2000.

Besides these companies, there were dozens, even hundreds, of others that had come along and were looking to make a quick $100 million or so. They sucked in investors and traders, especially when the Initial Public Offering would first come out. It wasn't unusual for the stock to go up a hundred points or more on the initial IPO day—and keep going up. It was an enormous game of musical chairs. The Nasdaq, which was the trading platform for almost all of these stocks, was predicted to replace the Dow or the S&P 500 as the new benchmark for the stock market.

Unbeknownst to any of us at the time, we were all part of a giant game of musical chairs. It was just a matter of time until the music stopped, the game ended, and we were all left without a chair. The Tech Bubble Burst, which would begin after the Nasdaq hit its peak in March 2000, would play out over the coming months and into 2001. That proved to be the beginning of my own bubble bursting.

They say bad things happen in threes. Personally, over the rest of the year, I would bear witness to this.

That February, early one morning, while sitting at the trading desk, I got an unusual call from my stepmother. My mom had passed away from cancer eleven years earlier, and my dad had met and married someone who turned out to be incredible in every way. She was everything my Dad needed after losing my mom . . . and also everything I needed. She had always said to me, "Please don't call me your stepmom . . . just call me Kathie." She went above and beyond to endear herself to me.

Her call to me was unusual not just because it was during trading hours (when she knew I had to concentrate on the markets) but in her tone. "Your Dad's not feeling well," she said, "We're going to the hospital. It's probably nothing to worry about. Maybe if you want to meet us there later..."

She was trying not to alarm me, but at the same time, this was all so out of character for her. I left the desk and went straight to the hospital.

Everything seemed fine when I got there. My dad and Kathie were both in good moods, even joking around. The doctors were performing tests on him to find out what was wrong. But as the day went on, things took a turn for the worse, and he had a series of heart attacks which weakened him more and more. By early evening, his body gave out, and he did not survive. It was a sudden loss that I did not see coming. Anyone who has ever lost anyone suddenly can relate.

When my dad passed away on that February day in 2001, he left everything to my stepmother; which I thought was fair. They had been together and married for almost ten years. I loved my stepmother, and she was genuinely a good person. I felt that it was right for him to take care of her. I was in my early thirties and had my own career and income. I didn't need anything.

In helping her figure everything out, he had various investments and retirement accounts . . . nothing substantial, but about $40,000 or so. He had been a senior vice president for Bankers Trust Company in NYC, which at one time was the seventh largest bank in the world. The bulk of his retirement account was through their plan. He had retired when my mom got sick with cancer years earlier. Because of his time and seniority, he had what we figured to be a substantial retirement account.

I remember growing up and watching him get up every morning by 5 a.m. to commute to the city. He had multiple choices for his commute from Point Pleasant Beach to New York City— either taking a bus, riding the train, or driving in a van pool with a group of fellow commuters. No matter which option he chose, it was a brutal two-plus hour ride each way. After working all day, he'd arrive home by 7:30 p.m., exhausted and usually not in the best mood from his long day. In addition, on many Saturdays, he had to go into his office to catch up on work that hadn't been completed during the week.

As a kid watching his father do nothing but work, it gave me an idea of what was required to support a family. He also told me many times that in order to make a decent living, I, too, would have to commute to the city. He explained that, in his view, our small community in central Jersey just couldn't provide a decent living. He was preparing me for what he saw as my future work life, which was what he was presently doing.

When I was first looking at a career in finance, I went on several interviews in the city and was offered different entry-level positions at a few firms. I imagined myself doing that commute every day as my father had done. I remembered his long, exhausting days. Something made me keep looking, and I ended up finding the options trader job that I took in Philadelphia.

Dad was quite bright, having worked his way up in the bank through the accounting division. I fully expected that my stepmother was going to be well taken care of—especially considering that she had just been diagnosed with cancer and would need to fall back on what was left to her. Bankers Trust had become Deutsch Bank, so there was a whole maze we had to go through to get answers. Finally, after many conversations with different people in their estate department, we learned about my dad's pension.

At the time of his retirement, his pension/401(k) had grown into a very substantial amount. The retirement planners from the bank went over the options with him:

1. He could take the full dollar amount and have it continued to be invested and managed by the people at the bank.

2. He could take over the account himself.... i.e., do a rollover into an Individual Retirement Account where either he or someone he hired would manage it.

3. He could "annuitize" it: turn it into lifetime income for himself and my mom.

The lady in the retirement office informed us that he had chosen number three. Furthermore, he had chosen a joint life annuity with himself and my mom. I reminded the lady that my mom had passed away over ten years ago in 1990, and my dad had recently passed and had left everything in his will to my stepmother. So now what happened?

"Nothing," was her response. My stepmother and I looked at each other.

"Okay, so how does she get his pension?" I asked her.

"She doesn't…there is no pension left. Your father had chosen to annuitize with his life and your mother's life only. Once they are gone, there is nothing left."

We were stunned. I asked the lady how this could have happened. I told her that my dad was very caring and would not have left my stepmother without anything from his pension. The lady could sense our anguish, and she explained further.

"Most people don't realize that they have other choices. Because they are so used to getting their paychecks while working, they are basically sold the idea that the only way to keep their steady paycheck is by annuitizing their pensions. I see it all the time. Sometimes they don't even realize to make it joint life. At least your dad did that with your mom. But once it's done, it is irrevocable. It can't be changed. I'm sorry, but there is nothing we can do."

I saw the hurt in Kathie's eyes and a feeling of helplessness.

Something inside me just knew that this was wrong. I didn't know it at the time, but this would be the catalyst that inspired me to do what I do . . . to not let a person's spouse and family be left with nothing.

Sadly, soon after losing my dad, Kathie was diagnosed with lung cancer. In order to get the best treatment possible, we agreed to make trips out to Fox Chase in Philadelphia. I was familiar with the area, having worked out there, and drove Kathie to the many doctor's visits over the coming months.

They told her that they had to remove her cancerous lung. If they didn't, she would die within a few months. Sitting there with her and hearing this directly from the surgeon, I felt myself losing my mind. But I had to stay strong for her and get her through this. She made the obvious decision to have the surgery. Her son flew in from California to be with her, too.

The surgery appeared to be a success. Not only did they get all the cancer, but she was expected to make a complete recovery. Kathie and I had become good friends in the time following my father's death. Through all of this, I was grateful still to have her love and wisdom in my life.

My stepbrother flew back home. I promised him that I would watch over his mom. I checked in on her every day. But in early July, she left me a cryptic voicemail saying that she was a little rundown and that she was going to be resting over the upcoming Fourth of July holiday.

I really didn't think anything of it. But by July 4, having not heard from her in a few days, I thought it best to take a ride to her house to check on her. She and my dad had been living in an adult community with a golf course, pool, clubhouse, and beautiful walking paths. My uncle came with me just in case she was sick and we needed to get a doctor, so I wouldn't have to do that by myself.

When we arrived and I unlocked the door, something wasn't right. There was that just that sense. We found her peacefully in bed having died in her sleep. I was devastated and collapsed on the ground while calling my aunt to report the news.

In the span of less than six months, I had lost the two people who represented my rock and foundation. Normally, like a lot of people, work would be a good distraction. But I felt myself not being able to concentrate. Add to the fact that with the tech bubble bursting, my super-sophisticated strategy of just holding positions until they went back up was no longer working. It was mutually agreed upon at the private equity firm that I should take time off. In a few weeks or months, I could come back. Yet somehow, I knew that I would not be back.

As long as I can remember, the Twin Towers of the World Trade Center had always held a special place to me. My Dad had worked at Bankers Trust Company in the building across the street, so growing up in the '70s, I had been through the towers many times to visit him. There was just something that resonated with me. I took many dates into the city and through the towers and even to Windows on the World Restaurant for dinners. The towers represented more than buildings to me. They represented everything good in the financial world, including my dad.

Thus, when they fell on September 11, even though I didn't lose anyone personally, I felt like I lost another part of me. This hurt. The fact that my dad worked there added to my pain. As 2001 drew to a close, I found myself at a point in my young life that I could never have imagined.

What happened on 9/11 impacted each of us individually. Those who lost family and loved ones had their added, indescribable pain. I found myself asking questions such as, "What do I want to do with my life?" Did I really want to sit behind a computer all day and make a living? Or was I supposed to do something else? I really didn't know. I even contemplated just taking a menial job that didn't require much thinking.

But I also remembered one of my favorite scenes in the movie Rocky when the future champ is chastised by his future manager Mickey for being a "leg-breaker for some cheap second-rate loan shark." Rocky replies almost sheepishly, "It's a living." Mickey glares back at him and shouts back, "It's a waste of life!" This one line stored in the back of my head somewhere was shouting to me to remind me to do more with my life.

The following year, I found myself wandering around in a bookstore, searching for something interesting to read. I came across a book in the business section called The Travelers Gift by Andy Andrews. I started thumbing through it and picked up on the main story: a person who seemed to be lost and, through God or something extraordinary, was taken back through history to learn from various life-changing figures we all know of to learn that he could also be transformed and change lives.

I bought the book and read it cover-to-cover in one night. This would impact my entire being and bring me out from the self-absorbed pity party that I had been having. It would cause me to find out what I was truly capable of and if I could really make a difference in my small community in central New Jersey.

As I reflected on what I wanted to do next, I kept going back to what had happened to Kathie despite my father's best intentions. Your loved ones should not be left with nothing due to a lack of planning or preparation.

I want to help you avoid such a jarring and sad outcome. Let's look at how to do that.

CHAPTER 2

Giants of Wall Street

The late 1970s and early '80s were a great time to be growing up "down the shore" in New Jersey. Besides all the culture that surrounded us, we lived within a couple of hours' drive from Philadelphia and New York City.

The New York Yankees were the dominant sports team, especially during their magical late '70s championship years. I watched every game I could, and went to as many games as possible to convince my dad or friends' dads to take me to. My favorite player was the heart and soul of that team, The Captain: Thurman Munson. I absolutely loved his tenacity and his will to win. A picture of him guarding the plate is forever stamped in my mind. He was everything athletically that I could only dream about emulating.

When he died in a horrific plane crash in August 1979, I found myself left with a void in sports that could not easily be filled. It no longer felt fun and exciting watching the Yankees—or almost any other sports, for that matter. I found myself asking, "What is the point of these games?" It's a sad thing to only be twelve years old and feel this way, but it was also what moved me toward the world of finance.

As a young kid who was so close to Wall Street, along with my dad working across the street from the World Trade Center, I was acutely aware of money and was drawn to some of the famous financial personalities of the time. These names didn't replace the heroes I had in sports like Munson, but for me, they did fill a void of interesting personalities.

One of the biggest names was Peter Lynch. He had taken over what at the time was a very small Fidelity Mutual Fund, which he grew into a legendary monster fund. His Magellan Fund was something so extraordinary that I remember his name sticking out from my dad and other adults talking about him with awe.

Mutual funds, in general, were really becoming the big thing to be invested in as 401(k)s became available. Most companies offered them as a big part of their retirement package. The funds were made up of either stocks or bonds, or a combination of the two. Sometimes they were made up of indexes like the S&P 500 Index. Even today, almost everyone who has worked for a company with a 401(k) plan has at least owned and had some knowledge of funds.

Another name from that period that stuck out as larger than life was Ivan Boesky. While not as likable as Peter Lynch, and for what turned out to be criminal financial dealings, Boesky was also a common name—especially in the '80s. The movie Wall Street paid special homage to him by using his words almost verbatim in Gordon Gekko's famous "Greed is Good" speech.

Boesky used a type of investment strategy known as arbitrage to take advantage of market inefficiencies that usually happened with a stock's price when a company was on the verge of being taken over by another company. By simultaneously buying the stock being taken over and shorting the company doing the takeover, there can be enormous profit potential from that investment. Obviously, it would help to know ahead of time which companies were on the verge of being taken over, which of course, is illegal. Boesky didn't think that was such a big deal. The SEC thought otherwise, and he was eventually charged and convicted of insider trading. Until he was caught, however, he was a respected and revered personality on Wall Street.

Many other names from that era defined the "greed" decade of the '80s. But there was one that stuck out to me beyond all the rest. Today, his name is not one that many would recognize . . .

When my dad commuted with a group of other bankers in a carpool van, they all got to be close friends. One of these guys worked for a company called Drexel Burnham Lambert. Over thirty years later, Drexel is just a blip on the radar. But at the time, it was The Gorilla in the room. Goldman Sachs had been and is still today the unquestioned leader in the investment world. But Drexel had positioned itself to take over and potentially dominate the investment world for the rest of the 20th Century. They were surpassing Merrill Lynch and Morgan Stanley and were within striking distance of Goldman.

One man had made that all possible, and he was nothing less than a savant when it came to investments and particularly what at the time was one small corner of the financial world . . . high yield bonds.

Michael Milken could take a 300-page prospectus of a new bond issue, figure out its future value to the fraction of a dollar, and then sell it on the street at a profit to the many customers lined up at his doors. In his early years, he would commute on a bus for 2.5 hours each way from Cherry Hill, New Jersey, to Wall Street and dissect these prospectuses and other financial documents during the whole ride. When it was too dark to read, he would use a miner's helmet with a big light in front.

I couldn't get enough of learning about Milken, and I would ask my dad and his commuting friend Vinnie from Drexel what was going on with this Wall Street titan and how he was able to figure out and own the bond market. Years earlier, Milken had left Cherry Hill and moved himself and his entire operation across the country to Los Angeles, where he opened a very discrete office and began to turn the financial world on its ear.

Of course, anyone who has studied financial history knows that Drexel and Milken were eventually convicted of numerous complex financial crimes, which led to Drexel collapsing and closing down and Milken going to prison. Even today, there's an argument that Milken's "crimes" were not crimes at all but rather the result of an overzealous prosecutor, which made him the ultimate scapegoat for the greed decade of the '80s.

But the idea of using bonds and bond-type investments was intriguing to me . . . the idea of a stock or mutual fund going up and the investor getting a return on their investment was what most are used to when we think of investments. The Peter Lynches of the world were doing this in a more complex way, and so were the Ivan Boeskys.

But Milken was using the bond market, particularly the high yield bond market—or junk bonds as they came to be known—as his main focus. There was something to this that clicked in my young mind back then: Not using junk bonds, but using fixed income investments to generate interest and dividends that also have the potential to grow. Even corporate bonds by themselves were not the way to go, but the right bond-type investments could be. Having a consistent income that is generated from dividends and interest rather than relying on stock or mutual fund gains while being subjected to potential losses could make all the difference to someone who needs to replace their paycheck.

Years later, I would learn to use Monte Carlo Simulations to project how long a retirement account can last and what chance someone had of not outliving their retirement. In most cases, it would show that by following their plan, the account would have a 70 percent or sometimes even 80 percent chance of lasting throughout life . . . which initially sounds great. But then I thought, "Wait, that's a 7 out of 10 or maybe 8 out of 10 chance of success. That's like playing Russian Roulette with your retirement, to still have a 20-30 percent chance of failure and of running out of money. How would that feel? Wouldn't it make sense to be at 100 percent or even 99.99 percent at the very least? By finding the least volatile, most consistent investments in the world featuring fixed income, could this be possible?" This would be the first piece of the puzzle of retirement planning that I would learn more about down the road.

CHAPTER 3

Going Too Far

W e've all heard the saying, "Money is the root of all evil." And most of us know and understand the full phrase: "For the love of money is the root of all evil," which comes from the Bible (1 Timothy 6:10).

The difference between each of these phrases obviously changes one's perception about money. I learned at a young age that money was simply a tool; its proper investment and use could make all the difference. My parents were conscious of this, and I was fortunate not to see any concept of a love for money.

It wouldn't be till I was starting out as an advisor working for Lincoln Financial Group that I would understand and absorb this. Through LFG, I was part of their educational workshop dinners, or what people typically know as seminars. In the early 2000s, we could get a group of over 100 retirees to attend these dinners. We would give them helpful information and offer them a free personal meeting to see if we could be of further help. Each attendee who wanted a meeting would fill in a basic information sheet with their investments and other assets. Sometimes, people would just check off the box for the free meeting and leave the rest blank. Usually, people were not worried about revealing their information, and they actually enjoyed bragging about how well they did. When someone left it blank, it usually meant that they had little to nothing to work with. Since I was new, I was naturally assigned to these folks, and it was up to me to meet with them and report back to the senior advisor if there was anything further to do.

The next day, I'm looking at one couple's information sheet to call them. I noticed that they live in Whiting, New Jersey, off Route 70, which isn't too far from my house in Toms River. I called and offered to come to their house if it was easier for them than to come to our office, which was in Sea Girt. I remember the wife chuckling and saying, "Oh, we don't have enough money to drive all the way to Sea Girt! We barely have enough to buy gas to get to the grocery store in Manchester." She did a great job of keeping my expectations as low as possible since this implied that if there was almost no gas money to get around, then there was most likely no money in investments, either.

Besides this comment, her overall demeanor on the phone gave me the impression that she and her husband were perennial "plate lickers" and attended multiple free seminars a week just for the free meal. Logically, I should have cut myself loose and let her go to enjoy more free dinners, but my instinct told me to try and make a meeting at their house. Something about her dismissive, cantankerous attitude was interesting to me, and I thought maybe

I could help them in some way, even if they had no investments to work with.

We had to work around their schedule of free lunches and dinners, but finally, we came to a day that worked. I promised to bring them Dunkin' Donuts as a gift for meeting with me. Looking back, I had no reason to go see these people, but at the time, I figured I had nothing to lose, and I'd gain some experience.

I stopped at Dunkin', picked up a big box of donuts and three large coffees, and followed Route 70 West as I had printed out directions to their house. The farther west I got, the more rural it became, and I was enjoying the ride that I used to take many times when I was younger heading to the Spectrum in Philadelphia to see a game or event.

I should not have been too surprised when I found myself suddenly turning off into a trailer park that I had almost passed by. The marketing companies that are used to mail out the free seminar invitations are supposed to exclude trailer parks because there is no real chance of the owners having any investible assets. But I would learn that this couple and many others would just get the info about the seminars from a friend who received the invite with a real house and then call in and attend themselves. I remember thinking, "Why not? If I'm older with a lot of free time, and not much money, why not go to a free dinner at a nice restaurant every night if I just have to listen to someone speak about money for an hour?"

Pulling into the trailer park, I saw that this was a pretty poor area. Most of the homes were in very bad condition, and some were probably lucky to still be standing after years of neglect and our New Jersey climate and weather taking their toll. I followed the road and reached the address of the couple. I sized up their trailer. While it wasn't as bad as some others that I had driven by, it was definitely not in good shape. I just remember broken things all around it . . . and a kind of sadness overtook me because of what was obviously a state of disarray.

I got out of my car. Juggling the donuts, coffees, and my briefcase, I went up to the door. Putting the coffees down on the broken step, I knocked since there was no doorbell anywhere. I heard the husband yell from inside, "Yeah, yeah….be right there!" It was the middle of summer and probably close to 90 degrees, but they had their windows open since air conditioning was not an option.

He opened the door and greeted me in a manner as cantankerous as the wife. "We don't usually end up meeting with any of you hucksters once we talk to you on the phone and you realize not to waste time, but Clare said you were bringing coffee and enough donuts for the week, so come on in and let's get this over with."

"Thanks, Joe," I replied as I stepped into their home and handed him his free donuts. As I came in and sat down at a table with mismatched broken chairs, I took a casual look around. I don't consider myself judgmental about people and their economic circumstances, but the sheer poverty that I saw around me was overwhelming. It reminded me of what I took for granted. In the scorching heat, with no AC from even individual units, there was a smell that they obviously were very used to. All around their home, there were just broken things everywhere. There were even holes in their floors where dirt and mud came through. The walls had peeling wallpaper that was so discolored, it had to be from the 1960s.

I actually had to work to hide my sadness. This couple was in their retirement years and should be enjoying life, traveling, and doing whatever they wanted. Yet here they were in the 21st Century United States with no air conditioning or any other "modern" conveniences. Sitting there with them, they both began to devour the donuts and coffee I had brought. "What a treat," Clare said in a tone that was finally at least a little friendly. But I didn't blame them for having a chip on their shoulders.

"So, what do you want to sell us?" Joe asked me in between bites as he worked on his second donut.

"Well, I have nothing to sell," I replied, "but it would be a pleasure to see if I can give you some helpful information that you can use yourselves if you'd like."

I really meant that. I knew that there was probably nothing I could do for them except maybe give them ideas on saving and budgeting.

"Okay . . . well, all right . . . You may need to give us another free dinner if this goes on too long. These donuts can only go so far," Joe replied as he started on his third one.

Rather than telling them anything that was probably useless to them, I began to ask them questions about themselves and their lives. They told me they had both worked in the local supermarket for all their lives. He was in the butcher department and she was a checkout person. They had six grown children whom they seemed to not like at all, and they retired a few years ago with no pensions or any other income except Social Security. They never went anywhere or did anything because of what they did for a living and having six kids. Now both in their late seventies and not in great health, they were thinking of returning to work to help pay their substantial medical bills that Medicare didn't fully cover.

The more I heard, the sadder I got. I would have no idea just how sad their story would become as they told of their children all being very successful, but pretty much abandoning them to live their own lives. Part of me could understand since the couple was so angry and unhappy, but I didn't fully see their children's point of not helping them at all. They had every profession covered— doctors, lawyers, engineers . . . I thought, "How could this be?"

As they went on and on about their medical bills and how it caused them not even to have air conditioning in 90-plus degree heat, I remembered something: the government had a program to help people in extreme poverty.

"Hey guys," I interjected as the lightbulb went off. "Have you at least looked into Medicaid?"

They looked at each other like I was from another planet.

"We don't have that option. It's too complicated to get that. But if you want to try and help us, then maybe we'll have enough to buy you some donuts!"

We all laughed, but I really thought that I was onto something here. With just a little help, they could be relieved of at least some of their medical bills through the Medicaid program that they should qualify for. I remembered that they needed to have virtually no liquid assets except maybe $2,000 in cash. Looking around their trailer, I was sure that they'd meet that requirement.

I asked them about any assets besides their trailer home. If they had any investments or any bank accounts—or anything, for that matter, with more than $2,000 in it. They looked at each other for a quick minute, then Joe said, "You want to see our stuff? Well, it's probably a waste of time, but you seem like someone we can talk to, so hang on . . ."

He went to another room, got an old cardboard box out, and brought it over to the broken-down table where we were seated. When someone hands you an old cardboard box, you never know what you'll find—especially regarding investments. I looked at them as I opened the box. They seemed to be watching me and waiting for my reaction.

I reached in and was relieved that there were only papers inside. Like I said, you never know what you'll be handed when it comes to these boxes. Over the years, clients have handed me stamp collections, baseball card collections, all sorts of coins, and old currency. I even had a box full of jewelry that the client swore was worth thousands of dollars, only to find out it was costume jewelry that was virtually worthless.

But these were all papers, and as I put them on the old broken table in front of me, I was surprised to see that they were legitimate investment account statements. I recognized various big-name brokerage houses, individual mutual funds, and equities.

There were also various insurance contracts and annuities. I looked up at the couple and almost got the sense that they were enjoying me struggling with all the statements. I shook my head and said to myself, "This doesn't make any sense." As I was going through it all, I saw numbers that were just astounding: $742,000, $855,000, $1.2 million. Each statement had larger numbers than the previous one.

I realized that something must be wrong. All these assets for this couple just did not add up. I checked the dates on the statements: They were all current. Then, I looked at the names on the statements. Joseph and Clare were on most of them together but there were also some IRAs that had just one name, which was either his or hers.

"These are all yours?" I asked.

"Well, who the hell else's would they be?" replied Joe in his cantankerous way.

Still dumbfounded, I got out my calculator and began to enter the numbers. I saw out of the corner of my eye that both Joe and Clare had almost smirks on their faces. After several minutes of adding everything up, I looked at the total on my calculator. I stared at both of them in utter disbelief. Did they have any idea what they have and what this can do for them? I felt a wave of sadness, wondering if they realized what they had and how it could have impacted their lives.

"Guys, do you realize. . .you have over SIX MILLION DOLLARS in assets here?"

They both looked at me like I had two heads.

"What the hell are you talking about?" Joe yelled.

I repeated the number so it could sink in. The sadness I felt was growing. My mind just kept asking, "How could people have so much and not even realize it?" I know numbers can be intimidating and confusing. Often, people over- or underestimate their net worth all the time. But to not even realize they had $6,000,000!

I saw Joe pull something out of his pocket. It was a slip of paper that he unfolded and reviewed. Then he looked at me and said, "You sure you added that up right?"

"Huh?" I asked. "What do you mean?"

"Well, the correct number is $6,248,395," Joe replied, almost spitting out the number with contempt.

"What???" I almost screamed.

I could not believe that not only did they know down to the penny exactly what they had, they also knew that I could not comprehend their situation.

"What do you mean 'what?' Here, these are the totals from everything."

He handed me his paper. On it, I saw each investment scribbled on a line and a number next to it. Down at the bottom was the total: more than $6.2 million.

I looked at them and they looked back at me incredulously. My sadness turned into genuine depression. I could not believe that these two intelligent people would have this amount of investible assets and be living the way they were. I've heard the stories of a homeless person on the street who had passed away with $100,000 in their shopping cart, but this is beyond that. How could something like this be happening?

This time Clare spoke up.

"We like to watch the numbers go up," she said. "We started saving when we first met almost sixty years ago. We saved for our marriage. Then we saved to have a family. Then we saved for our retirement. We never spent. We never did anything or went anywhere. We started with nothing. We thought eventually we might need it so we never spent it on anything. We just got used to living without. And here we are almost sixty years later."

I didn't know what to say, so I went back to numbers, which I do when I don't understand something.

"But guys, the bank CDs are currently paying over 5 percent (this was around 2006), so if you had it all in FDIC insured accounts you could be making over $300,000 a year with no risk. That's the worst case. But you're mostly in equities and equity funds, and I'm seeing your returns are well above that."

Joe cut me off.

"You don't understand. We came from nothing and grew up during the Depression. We just started saving, so eventually we could do whatever we want. But what we want is to just keep saving."

I tried to make sense of what this almost eighty-year-old man was telling me.

"So you're doing this for your family. You're saving for your four sons."

That would explain everything. There are many people out there who will do without for themselves their whole lives just so their heirs can live better.

"No, we don't even like our sons. They are all well off anyway, and they don't want or need anything from us."

"So you're just saving because…"

"We told you. . .Because we like to watch the numbers go up. Now you can help us make them go up even more."

I don't know why or how, but at that moment they decided to make me their advisor on all of their assets: $6.2 million. They became my biggest client at that point and to this day one of my biggest clients.

When I left their trailer, I should have been thrilled to have landed such a large account. But I was anything but thrilled. The sadness I felt earlier had intensified. I found it implausible that people could work and save their whole adult lives … almost sixty years … and have nothing to show for it but a bunch of statements with numbers.

Here these folks were, close to the end of their lives. They had revealed to me the health issues they were both dealing with, too. They had saved and could do just about anything they wanted: travel or anything else that their hearts desired. They had children and grandchildren to possibly leave a legacy for. But none of that mattered. Watching the numbers go up was all they wanted, even to the point of living in a trailer that was falling apart.

My mind could not comprehend this. As I drove home, I kept thinking of the words to a popular '80s song by the Thompson Twins: King for a Day.

I've heard it said . . . or maybe read . . . only money makes the world go 'round.

But all the gold . . . won't heal your soul . . . if your world should tumble to the ground.

CHAPTER 4

Getting Punched in the Mouth

W hen I moved from the world of options trading to becoming a financial advisor, I was introduced to what I thought at the time were very exciting simulations that take everything into account upon retirement to calculate the predicted success rate of a financial plan.

These Monte Carlo Simulations were first widely used in the middle of the 20th century and gained prominence by the 1980s and '90s for their accuracy. The theory is that if you can put together a plan, with a combination of equities, bonds, and mutual funds, and get the success rate up to more than 80 percent, you have an eminently viable retirement plan in place. All you had to do was follow the plan, and everything would work out great. Thousands of financial advisors and stockbrokers, along with their clients, followed these plans and everything worked.

Mike Tyson said it best: "Everyone has a plan until they get punched in the mouth." In 2008, these advisors and millions of retirees got punched in the mouth. The markets crashed, and with the lost decade of financial growth, many had to go back to work doing things they could never have imagined just to pay their bills.

How could this have happened, and how were so many wrong when it came to financial planning? We know over the long run, the market always comes back. We saw this in 2008, and we saw it more recently in 2020. But why were retirees wiped out? It would help to look at the "plan" they were following so carefully before the stock market punched them in the mouth.

For more than one hundred years, the consensus has been that the average return of the stock market has been about 10 percent, depending on whether dividend reinvestment is taken into account.[1] Even if you conservatively estimate an 8 percent return and then plug equity-based investments into a portfolio, it should be safe to say that a withdrawal rate of 4-6 percent is more than fair.

If the total retirement account totaled $1 million dollars, under this plan, you should be able to take out $40-60k each year and not even have the principle go down at all. Having come from the world of options trading, this all made sense to me back in the early-mid 2000s.

I actually had a couple named Ted and Sue come to one of my dinner seminars that I did in 2007 and show me this exact plan that their advisor had put together with them. Ted's IRA alone was worth well over $1 million, and Sue's was over $400,000. Their

---

[1] James Royal, PH.D., Arielle O'Shea. NerdWallet. December 8, 2022. "What Is the Average Stock Market Return?" https://www.nerdwallet.com/article/investing/average-stock-market-return

plan was about 200 pages of charts and graphs, and scenarios . . . all with great detail and color. My prospective clients were very impressed with all of this, and I must admit, so was I! I found the information very compelling, and even though it wasn't my plan, I had to congratulate them on being in what seemed to be such a good place financially. I could only offer to be available if their advisor were to retire.

They walked out of my office proud of themselves. I thought they had every right to be . . . to this day, I always feel that if someone is either doing as good or a better job than I can do, whether working with an advisor or doing it themselves, then I really can't add any value. I'd rather just congratulate them and leave on good terms than try and tear apart a good plan. People can see through that anyway. I really never expected to hear from them again . . . even after 2008 when the markets crashed, I figured that if they are only withdrawing 4-6 percent, they'd be able to "weather the storm."

Three years passed. I took their call and heard Ted speak. It was not the same confident and proud voice from our first encounter.

"Bill . . . I got to tell you . . . Sue and I really appreciated how fair you were with us when we saw you after your seminar a few years ago. You remember that you said you thought we had a good plan, and our advisor did a great job in setting it up for us?"

"Yes, I do . . . but I'm sensing you've had some issues since the market crash?"

"Issues would be an understatement. We'd like to come in and see you again, and maybe this time you could really help us."

I liked this couple a lot and remembered them well, so I was glad that they wanted to come back in. I was also very curious as to what was going on with their "plan."

They arrived the next day and got right to the point.

"Bill, the plan we showed you that we were following has imploded. We've lost over 60 percent since the market crashed. Our advisor kept telling us to follow the plan, but because we lost so much in the crash, our income eats into the principal every month. So even with the market going up now, our retirement accounts are going down."

I understood the idea of what was happening to them . . . it is described as reverse-dollar cost averaging. I listened to Ted go on and Sue concurred that they were both at a loss and seemed to not be getting any guidance from their advisor.

Rather than pile on and add to their anguish, I explained what was happening to them. I reminded them that when they were working and contributing to their 401(k)s, they were adding money to them every month. It was the same amount each month, but it actually didn't buy the same number of investments. Because the market had gone up and down, they had been dollar-cost averaging into their investments. Obviously, when the market was up, like it was for most of the '80s and '90s, their accounts were up, and they were thrilled. But when the markets were down, and their accounts were down, they may not have been as happy, but they were actually able to buy more funds because each fund's share cost less. They were on sale, as Warren Buffet would say. The market comes back in the long run, and they had bought some shares at discounted prices. So when it was all said and done, and they were set to retire, they experienced exponential growth like so many people who accumulated in their retirement accounts in the '80s and '90s. When they retired, with the market doing what it did, they had every right to expect continued financial success following their plan.

But now that they are no longer contributing and are actually taking money out every month (taking income), the opposite is happening. Reverse-dollar cost averaging is taking place, and now they're in a difficult position. No matter what happens in the market, they can't stop the bleeding unless they make some changes.

Giving them this basic knowledge was actually empowering to them. Their advisor, with all his charts and graphs and plans, was never prepared to be "punched in the mouth." But in all fairness, who is?

I ended up sitting with them for a long time. I went into the world of conservative investments and how—while they couldn't fully be where they had been before the crash—there was still time to do things to fix the damage and right the ship.

I showed them the universe of investment options. This sounds like something that could take many hours or days to explain. In reality, when you chunk it all down, there are only about a dozen different types of investments that are available to everyday Jersey people. I think the financial industry likes to make things more complicated. I tell my clients that this gives a lot of folks jobs and careers just to be able to decipher all the information for everyone else.

The investment world is divided into two categories. The first is what most are familiar with: mutual funds, equities, and other choices based on the market. Most everyone who worked for a big company has had a 401(k) consisting of these. This is how wealth was accumulated over the years, especially in the '80s and '90s when the market was on a tear.

The second category is filled with more conservative investment choices. They include bonds and bond-type vehicles that provide interest and dividends. While bonds themselves are yielding much lower interest than even just a few years ago, there are other options such as preferred stocks that can provide a 4-6 percent dividend for income or reinvestment.

It also helps to look at the history of the stock market for the last 100-plus years. Most people have heard of "bull" and "bear" markets. They know that a bull market means the market is going up like we saw in the '80s and '90s. In fact, from 1982-2000, even with mini crashes during that period, we had the longest bull run on record. For eighteen years, you could be blind and throw a dart at a board full of investments, and anywhere the dart landed would have worked. I know this because like I said before, having traded options in the '90s and experiencing so much success, I thought I was brilliant. Well, I wasn't brilliant; I was just in a market where as long as I bought and held, I would win. This is where "buy and hold" comes from . . . this became the stockbroker's mantra: "Just hang on; it will come back."

The problem, of course, with that thinking is what we learned in 2000 when the tech bubble burst, and most of those stocks never came back. Those who invested in those stocks and the Enrons and others lost everything. We had the "lost decade," as it was called because if you invested in the market in 2000, by 2010, you would have made zero.

We all lived through that pain and experienced it firsthand. But to think that a lost decade was bad, what about a lost two and a half decades? Look further back in history to almost one hundred years ago to the 1920s and the market run-up during that time. Suddenly, in October 1929, the stock market crashed, and the Great Depression started. What most don't realize, and what I alluded to, is that if you had invested at the peak of the market before the crash, it would take twenty-five years, not for your investment to grow, but rather for it to be finally worth what you had started with. To put it another way, $100,000 or $1 million would not be worth $100,000 or $1 million again until 1954! This is incredible when we think about the fact that we had to go through all that time in the Depression and the years that followed it, up to and including World War II and the Korean War, and finally almost half a decade into the 1950s.

By looking at history, we can learn not to repeat its mistakes. There are so many investment advisors and financial planners out there with only good intentions. But I think for many people, these advisors are leading them towards Niagara Falls; only no one can see the actual Falls until it's too late. Like with Ted and Sue, no matter how good or detailed their "plan" was, it was broken.

Granted, if the markets were only going up like in the '80s and '90s, then those Monte Carlo Simulations are wonderful. The problem is that none of us know where the market is going tomorrow or next month or next year. Who could have thought after COVID-19 erupted in March 2020 and the market crashed that over the next year it would make and keep making all-time highs?

When Ted and Sue became my clients, the first thing they asked me for was my plan. What could I do for them? And what type of plan do I have that can work in any market?

This is what separates true retirement planning from just investment management, and this is where we go into the heart of what needs to be done to make it all work.

CHAPTER 5

"It's Different This Time"

The idea that it is possible to actually generate consistent income from your accounts without being subject to market volatility sounds almost foreign to the way most of us have thought while we worked and added to our accounts.

I remember something a good friend told me in 2007: he wanted to invest and grow his account. He told me that he didn't mind the risk. In fact, he was willing to take enormous risk for the growth potential that he was looking for. Like me, he was in his early forties at the time and said he had a lot of years to go before retirement, so he didn't mind the market fluctuations.

Accordingly, we set up a portfolio of mutual funds and equities that were designed to take advantage of what we both thought would be a continuous booming market. After all, the market had crashed pretty hard in the earlier part of the decade, and now things were different. The belief was "clear sailing ahead."

The first thing we should always be careful of is when they say, "It's different this time." We know what happened in 2008. When the market crashed hard, my friend lost over 50 percent of his account value. I remember thinking to myself that this was horrible. I had also lost considerable amounts in my own investments at the time, but for my friend to have lost also made it even worse. I finally understood the stories of brokers and advisors jumping out of windows after market crashes because they were so ashamed of losing their client's money.

My friend was beside himself. He did not realize that the market could go down so hard and wipe out half or more of many people's accounts. Few realized that. While my friend and I were both young enough to recover and come back from our losses, I remember thinking how fortunate I was to have stayed on the more conservative side for my clients who were at or nearer to retirement.

It got me wondering, "Is there a way for someone to invest for retirement income without leaving themselves exposed to the market?"

Usually, when you look for something, you'll find it somewhere surprising. In this case, I was looking for the safest, most conservative investment available. Of course, I found my answer in the least obvious place, which is the most aggressive form of investing: options.

Options can best be described as using enormous leverage to invest. One option contract controls one hundred shares of the underlying asset. Having traded options in the 1990s, I had a good feel for just what that leverage meant . . . good and bad. In some cases, the investor could be exposed to unlimited loss. In other words, not just everything invested in the option, but also everything in the account and potentially everything owned. This is what it means to sell naked calls and puts. When you're the seller of the option, you are contractually obligated to cover the trade at any time the buyer of the option (who is on the other side of the trade) desires. This can put unsuspecting investors or brokers in an untenable position. When the investment goes in the wrong direction, and the investor has leveraged their positions with options and did not hedge or protect themselves, they potentially lose everything. So how can options be part of an investment strategy?[2]

On the other side of the options trade is the buyer of the option. You can pay an amount for the underlying stock to go up and if the stock goes up, you win exponentially because holding the option on the stock means you potentially control 100 shares for a very small amount of investment.

For example, say we wanted to invest in the market, and we choose the S&P 500 Index, which represents the 500 largest publicly traded companies in the U.S. Thus, we buy an option in this index or the SPY as the symbol is called that we use. We believe that the market is going to go up 20 percent in the next year or so. We could buy an option in the S&P Index that expires in about a year for maybe $5 for each share, which times 100 equals $500. In other words, for $500, if the market goes up like

---

[2] This is intended for illustrative purposes only and should not be construed as advice. Investing in options involves risk, including the loss of more than the initial investment. Carefully consider your personal situation before investing.

we believe or even more, our option pays off big. What happens if the market doesn't go up, or actually goes down? What if it goes down 20 percent or even more? What do we lose? How bad is it?

You may already know that all we lose is our investment of $500. Theoretically, our profit potential is unlimited. Imagine buying options in the stock market in April of 2020 that expired a year later. That's the power of buying options. You can always control how much you will lose.

Of course, no one can predict when the market (and in turn, the S&P 500 Index) will go up. If you could, then you wouldn't be reading this book or need anyone else's help for that matter. But what if you could do something else that would offset the times when the market didn't go up or went down—or even crashed?

In order to do that, you have to use other fixed-income investments. There are quite a few to pick from, including bonds and bond-type vehicles. But in order to provide the safety that is recommended, the investment we would use would be in our own country in the form of U.S. Treasury Bonds.

You may already be aware that Treasuries come in the form of Bills, Notes, and Bonds. The difference between each of these is basically their timeframe. Treasury Bills have a short-term duration and mature in one year or less. Treasury Notes have a longer maturity of up to ten years. Treasury Bonds go out to thirty years before maturing.

Bills, Notes, and Bonds typically have lower yields, and on almost all occasions, the shorter the duration, the lower the yield. Then why would these even be considered as a viable investment option when the return is theoretically not keeping up with inflation?

To be clear, buying U.S. Treasuries by themselves is not a good investment. Yes, they may be "safe" based upon the credit worthiness of the United States Treasury. If the U.S. Treasury were to default on its debt, then it would be unprecedented and would make all the turmoil in the world seem like a walk in the park. We're left with the following question: With virtually no risk but also no return that keeps up with inflation, then what is their use?

One strategy is to provide what we call a hedge to offset the options in place to obtain the market's growth. This way, the interest from the Treasuries, while admittedly anemic, will cover the expense of the options.

If done correctly, if the market stays flat or goes down or even crashes, the options will expire worthless and the interest from the Treasuries will cover their cost, so the account will either be flat or possibly even still earning a bit of interest. This is in a flat or bad market year. In a worst-case scenario, such as another 2008, an account set up like this would actually not lose anything. Why? The options expired worthless, and the Treasuries covered the cost of these options. In 2008, for example, your account may not have lost at least 30 to 60 percent the way almost everyone's did. You could have been flat or maybe even up a little because the Treasuries earned more than enough interest to cover the cost of the options.

What happens when the market goes up? Now the real fun begins. We can buy options that are counting on the market going up, and we also buy more Treasuries to cover the cost of the options. Let's say the market goes up 20 percent. Those options will grow in value exponentially. Remember, because we had to buy Treasuries, we didn't put everything in the options for the market to go up. Still, what we did invest worked out to give us a nice return . . . and our Treasuries gave us a little bit too. Perhaps we earned a total of 12 percent from all of our investments, which may at first seem like we got shortchanged in a 20 percent market year. But remember: there was virtually no risk to get whatever return the options provided.

A final piece to this portfolio would be adding bond-type investments to further offset the years when the market is down. Corporate bonds or bond funds are not paying any type of viable return at the moment. They may yield a little more than Treasuries, but now there is real risk that the company could default. We all remember Enron, WorldCom, and Lucent. No one could have predicted their demise, but if you invested in these companies, you basically lost your entire investment. If you were a debt holder and bought bonds issued by them, then at best, you only lost 95 percent! Therefore, why take any risk with companies by holding their bonds?

A better option might be other bond-type investments called preferred stocks or "preferreds." Like bonds, they are issued by corporations. Instead of paying interest, they pay dividends, usually on a quarterly basis. These preferreds are a hybrid between common stocks (which most are familiar with) and bonds. Their price doesn't fluctuate like common stock, and it has what's called a par value, like bonds. It will stay close to its par value depending on a few variables.

We wouldn't buy just any company's preferred stocks. We would use companies such as major banks and financial institutions. Over the years, I've used Goldman Sachs, JP Morgan, Chase Bank, Bank of America, and others, for their preferreds. I tell my clients "Love 'em or hate 'em, these banks are probably not going anywhere, so why not take advantage of what they offer with their preferreds?" When used properly and not excessively, these bank-issued preferred stocks can bring the annual return up during down market years.

By using these components in the right quantities, you can set up a portfolio that could provide consistent income for the rest of your life and beyond. If one spouse passes away, the income would continue for the other. And when God calls both spouses home, the income could continue for the descendants if so desired, thus leaving a lasting legacy.

Now the question is whether to do this on your own or to get professional help? Let's explore further...

CHAPTER 6

The 4 Percent Rule

You've probably heard of the 4 Percent Rule. Here in some New Jersey towns, people may think it means the limit on how high our property taxes can go up each year.

I'm just kidding. Actually, thanks to the Senior Freeze, many folks do not have their property taxes go up, or they get refunded if they do rise.

When it comes to retirement planning, the 4 Percent Rule has been around for quite a while. Old-school investment advisors seem to love it. The rule simply states that as long as you take out no more than 4 percent of your total retirement assets each year, there's a very good chance that you will never run out of money. Certain advisors love to run these Monte Carlo analyses, which show that you would have as much as a 90 percent chance of success by adhering to the 4 Percent Rule.

That sounds great! Or does it?

Back in the early 2000s, when new clients would proudly come in with the 4 Percent Rule from their previous advisor, I would usually say something like, "You're right. Ninety percent is a pretty good percentage. And if we went down to Atlantic City together and there was a game that offered 90 percent odds or even 70-80 percent odds, I bet we'd play that game all day, right?"

The clients would all say yes, and some would even be excited, thinking I was inviting them down to Atlantic City for the day. ☺

But then I would say, "How many times are you retiring?"

They would give me a strange look and pretty much say 'Once,' unless they were going to start a new hobby that could turn into an income. I would then point out, "If you only have one time to retire and one time to get it right, wouldn't it be like having a gun loaded with one bullet and playing Russian Roulette?"

This would usually shock them, and I would be careful to remind them that I'd never expect them to really do this. But I want to make sure they understand the seriousness of risking their future years and having even a 5 or 10 percent chance of failure.

Again, this was during the early part of the 2000s. We had not yet experienced the market crash of 2008 or the ensuing "lost decade," which showed no gains in the stock market for over a ten-year period. When you are working and adding to your retirement accounts, you can actually dollar-cost average into your investments. We know that by dollar-cost averaging over time, compound interest can happen. Let's say you have ABC stock or fund and it's worth $10. You have $100 to invest so you can buy ten shares at $10 each. Next month, ABC goes up to $12. Once again, you only have $100 to invest. The higher price means this time you can only buy 8.3 shares. The following month, the price drops to $7, and your account goes down. You're not happy about your investment going down, but for that same $100 investment, you're able to buy over fourteen shares.

Imagine this goes on month after month, year after year, until one day you retire, and you've accumulated thousands of shares of ABC at various prices. Your dollar-cost averaging has produced an enormous next egg for your retirement. It's a beautiful thing when you consider that fundamental process along with the power of compound interest over the years.

As you reach retirement, you or an advisor has put together a plan that follows the 4 Percent Rule. Instead of adding, you're taking out 4 percent a year. Some years the market is up, but sometimes it is down. Sometimes, like in 2008, it's even down substantially. What happens then? You're doing reverse dollar-cost averaging and exposing yourself to the possibility of running out of funds over the course of your retirement.

Does that sound hard to believe? It shouldn't be. Right after the financial crisis in 2008, I remember sitting with new retirees who were shellshocked because while the market was down "only" 40 percent, their account was down over 70 percent. Why? Because they were taking money out. It's a terrible lesson to have to learn and realize too late. That is why we need to rethink the whole 4 Percent Rule—or adjust the "rule" to make it work.

Let's explore some ideas . . .

The big question is: "What can be done to make sure that you never run out of money?" Is there something or some investment that can "guarantee" you don't run out?

The insurance industry tried to answer that question with these complex annuities and offering annuitization options. This may sound good, but what this means is that if you have a lump sum of, say, $500,000 and you annuitize that money, you no longer have your lump sum, but rather a guaranteed lifetime monthly or annual income from it. The income can never run out while you're alive. That sounds good so far, doesn't it?

But what if something changes down the road and you need some or even all of your lump sum of money? What if there is an emergency, and you call up the insurance company or the person who sold you this annuity and tell them you have a dire situation and need a big part of your $500,000? They'll tell you, "Sorry, you can only get your monthly income. There is no lump sum available." How can this be? It's YOUR money, after all. Well, it was. Now it's an annuity that you are stuck with and can't get out of or change.

As if that's not bad enough, let's say you had an accident. You're out skydiving or hang-gliding, you fall to Earth, and God calls you home. You had this annuity for yourself and your spouse that was supposed to pay for everything for the rest of your life. Your spouse calls up the insurance company to change the payments to her. Instead of that happening, she receives a condolence letter saying something like, "Sorry about your loss. But we can't change the monthly income payments to your name because once your husband passed away, they ended." Now, instead of leaving your spouse financially secure, they have nothing. The insurance company keeps all the rest. It's horrible, but it happens often, all because of these companies and annuity salesmen preying on people's fears.

What if there was another way? What if there was a way to have your cake and eat it, too? In other words, to have your lump sum investment, available anytime, and also have a monthly income stream that is guaranteed for life? What if, when God calls you home, your spouse and family would still have the lump sum that they can take and do with whatever they want or need? And all this was guaranteed? Well, this is possible . . . [3]

A few years ago, some good people in the financial industry realized that this situation was untenable. There had to be some way to supply what was needed. They came up with using a certain type of tax-sheltered annuity that didn't have all the complications or expenses or moving parts and created a simple income benefit from it that was guaranteed. This may cost a small fee (though sometimes there is no fee), but this became what is now known as a GMIB . . . Guaranteed Minimum Income Benefit.

Not only is the account still there and still whole, but this GMIB can be set up for one or both spouses. In many cases, the lifetime income that this can provide can be far more than 4 percent. Sometimes, it can be 5, 6, or 7 percent—or even higher. And it never runs out for both the account holder and their spouse. When God calls you and your spouse home, your family gets every

---

[3] Annuity guarantees rely on financial strength and claims-paying ability of issuing insurance company. Annuities are insurance products that may be subject to fees, surrender charges and holding periods which vary by carrier. Annuities are not FDIC insured.

penny that is left in the account. You really do have the best of both worlds with this.

There are many bad choices out there. This can actually be one thing that can be a wise choice and make so much sense. For many of the families that I help, they rely on this lifetime income. I remind them that it's not William Skillender Wealth Management that is guaranteeing their income, but rather a multi-billion-dollar insurance company that provides this guarantee. Knowing their income is there, their lump sum is there, and their legacy for their family is there is priceless for families. It takes all the stress and guesswork out of trying to figure out if there will still be income there in twenty or thirty years or more.

My oldest client just celebrated her one-hundredth birthday. I joke with Lillian that she will probably still be here for ten-or twenty years. She doesn't think so, but if she is, her income will be, too. She doesn't get out and party like she used to, but at least in this one area of life, she is living stress-free.

When this type of account is combined with other investments from the world of fixed income, it creates a can't-lose situation.

CHAPTER 7

Let's Summarize . . .

. . . where we're at so far . . .

When it comes to investing for retirement, the conventional thought by many brokers and investment advisors is to get the most gains from the assets over time. By doing so, income from these gains can be used to potentially provide a comfortable lifestyle.

What we've learned, however, is that something like the 2008 market collapse can happen, which will potentially be catastrophic to this type of retirement planning.

The idea of using the world of fixed income investments where we're getting dividends and interest instead of gains (or potential losses) is actually the shift that is needed to generate consistent income. That would feature a combination of investments, which could be income bond-type holdings such as preferred stocks, along with longer-term treasuries that are backed by the credit worthiness of the federal government (which in the modern day may feel a little less secure than in previous times). Combine these with certain options in the various market indexes and a portfolio can be created that provides much more consistent income than trying to rely on the returns of the stock market.

The idea of constructing this portfolio may seem exciting and challenging. And there is a sense of pride in doing it yourself by taking the time to learn about options and how they work through leverage. You're also able to have full control over your investments. I understand that way of thinking and can very much relate to it. Let me go back to my days on the options trading desk of a private equity firm back in the 1990s . . .

I first learned about options as a way to use leverage to potentially make a lot more return on a small investment when the underlying asset (stock) moves up or down. I was trained by some seasoned traders who had been trading for decades. The markets were different back then. For one thing, stocks traded in fractions . . . ¼ , ½, etc. That meant market moves on stocks were more pronounced. In my years of trading, I thought I had learned it all. I became proficient at the use of this leverage and eventually could actually hold my own trading with the pros.

Fast forward almost ten years to studying for my securities license. I was told by the people bringing me into the industry at Lincoln Financial that options would need to be a major part of my studying and thus a big part of the exam. Naturally, I figured that this would be a walk in the park for me since I had so much experience actually trading.

I was almost going to skip the options material altogether but then thought, let me at least take the practice quizzes so I can remind myself that I got this all down. Well, you may guess that I was in for a rude awakening. I remember the first question describing a complex options formula that I had no clue as to what it meant. I figured that it must be an anomaly and that the rest of the practice questions would be more along the lines of what I was experienced with. But each succeeding question was harder than the previous one. Here I was thinking I was so proficient and almost dismissing it as a waste of my valuable study time Yet I was facing these questions like they were in another language. I couldn't believe that my knowledge from actively trading options amounted to nothing. I got only about 30 percent of these questions correct—pretty humbling for an "options trading expert," right?

As the old saying goes, I had a lot to learn. Fortunately, I realized that I would have to put time into studying options. I can't remember how many hours it turned out to be, but it was the most intense part of my time preparing, and it ended up being the most intense part of my exam.

After it was all said and done, I passed my Series 7 Securities exam on the first try with a respectable score of 83. I know that all the time I put into the options section proved significant in helping me pass.

So now, what does all this have to do with you possibly studying all there is to learn about options and the other pieces of a retirement plan, putting all the pieces together, and doing it yourself successfully? Maybe it's something that even if you spent weeks or months learning everything there is to learn and then actually trading options live, it just may be one of those things where it would be worth it to have someone doing the work for you. It's a bit like putting an addition on your house or rebuilding the transmission in your car: you could possibly learn and do it yourself, but maybe it would be better to have someone else who already has years or even decades of experience do it for you.

Back in the '90s, when I was trading options, there was a famous (or rather infamous) commercial on television at the time. It seemed to be on constantly, especially on CNBC, which our trading desk (as most all traders did at the time) had on in the background.

The commercial starts off with a young guy who is in his senior year in high school looking over his options for college. He's excited as he's going through multiple acceptance letters and clearly understands that he is very fortunate to have so many choices of attending some of the finest universities in the nation. You see him smiling and going through them all, and then he grabs one and looks at it, and becomes even more happy and excited. Apparently, he has found his ideal choice of higher education, and now you see him exiting his bedroom and heading downstairs to tell his family whom he imagines will be just as thrilled.

He gets to the bottom of the stairs and sees his mom and dad are both there with funny looks on their faces. In his excitement, he doesn't notice their faces but is just thrilled to share his news . .

.

"Hey guys! I've found the college that I'm going to go to . . . Mom and Dad, thank you for helping me save up for this and have all my school paid for . . ."

The Mom looks at her son with a crooked smile and replies, "Sorry Mikey, but you're not going to go to college after all."

The son looks back and is both confused and dejected. "I'm not???"

"Nope. Somebody decided to try a little day trading" she replies as she looks knowingly at the father who sits sheepishly in front of his computer screen and turns around and says to the son a line that to this day is still in my head: "I thought it'd be fun!"

And the commercial ends with the son looking ever so sad and the father looking at his wife and son just like, "Oh well. Sorry about that." Then the logo for one of the larger investment firms appears on the screen with the message: Call us for professional advice.

That commercial, while very corny and silly, definitely resonated with the audience of do-it-yourself day traders back in the 1990s. Everyone thought they could make a fortune buying and selling stocks like Amazon and Yahoo. But there's a reason why most of the best traders and investment managers spend years if not decades pursuing their craft. If "everyone" could actually do it, then they would, and there would be no need for professionals. The problem is, and was back in the '90s, that opening a self-managed trading account and then initiating trades is relatively easy. If you can push a couple of buttons or point and click, you're a trader. But the truth is that investing and trading successfully while using the right combinations of the types of investments to put together the portfolio that is needed to produce consistent results for one's own account is just not feasible.

It would be like one of the top attorneys in the nation needing legal help and then choosing to represent himself or herself in a civil or criminal case. That just doesn't happen. They go out and find the right attorney who specializes in the field that they need help in. This would work the same for doctors or any other professional vocation. They seek out and utilize the absolute best that is available to them to do exactly what needs to be done.

There are thousands of financial advisors in New Jersey. Most of them are reputable and look to do what is best for their clients. While the financial industry does have its share of bad apples that can give it a bad reputation, for the most part, we are made up of honest, hard-working men and women who will go above and beyond for their clients and client families.

What, then, makes up the right specialist that could be the expert needed to put together the right portfolio and thus the right plan for you?

Let's explore that further . . .

CHAPTER 8

What About Reverse Mortgages?

If you own your home here on the Jersey shore, you've probably thought about or even already engaged someone about a reverse mortgage. The concept of using our home, which for many is our biggest asset, and getting either a lump sum of cash from it or a monthly income check for life—and never having to pay it back—can be very attractive. You just have to pay the taxes and normal upkeep and continue to live in your home.

I remember thinking in my thirties and forties that this seemed like a no-brainer. I figured my normal mortgage would be paid off and it would be great to take out a new mortgage that I wouldn't have to make a monthly payment on. I've met with many retirees and clients who have already done this and are very happy with this arrangement. For them, it works and has given them additional income.

For some, it may be a good thing. But if you haven't done a reverse mortgage and are considering it, let's explore a little deeper into the concept. There are many possible benefits to going this route, especially if there is a real shortfall in income from Social Security, pensions, and investments. But if you have not yet done this or are considering this, here are some things to consider:

Some people suggest taking the funds from the reverse mortgage and using them to invest. On the surface, this may sound like a good idea. Many stockbrokers and financial advisors will point out that over the last 100-plus years, the market has averaged 10 percent a year in returns.[4] So why not use the funds that may cost 4-5 percent from a reverse mortgage or even 3 percent from a conventional mortgage to make 8-10 percent? Over the past decade prior to writing this book, the market is closer to 15 percent.[5]

Here's the thing: Averages, like most statistics, can be deceiving. I like to tell a goofy story that illustrates this point: A wife drags her husband to the doctor because she's worried about his health. The doctor goes through his exam and asks the husband if he's doing anything for exercise. The husband responds, "Well, between my wife and I, we jog an average of ten miles a week." The doctor looks at him, surprised, and says "Wow! That's very good!" The wife happens to be in the waiting room and overhears this and barges into the exam room and exclaims, "Ha! He's saying we jog an average of ten miles a week between us because I go out and do

---

[4] James Royal, PH.D., Arielle O'Shea. NerdWallet. December 8, 2022. "What Is the Average Stock Market Return?" https://www.nerdwallet.com/article/investing/average-stock-market-return

[5] Rebecca Lake. Sofi. July 22, 2022. "What Is the Average Stock Market Return?" https://www.sofi.com/learn/content/average-stock-market-return/

twenty miles a week while he sits on the couch all day eating pizza and hot dogs!"

Although this is kind of a silly story, it does point out that averages, like most statistics, can be deceptive sometimes—including ones having to do with average stock market returns. While the market has averaged 8-10 percent, there have been long stretches where it has done zero or even negative returns. We already talked about the lost decade of the first part of the 21st century. We also pointed out that when the market crashed in 1929, it took twenty-five years for someone invested to get back to where they were—not even to grow a dollar but just to get back to even. When you take this into account and that a rising market is probably not going to sustain its average returns, then using borrowed funds in any form to invest can be very detrimental to one's retirement plan.

Besides the potential risks involved, the other thing that a reverse mortgage does is limit your future choices. Here's what I mean: while the idea of staying in your home forever and not paying a mortgage anymore while "cashing in" for the value can be appealing at the moment, you never know what can change down the road. Some of my clients have had major life events occur where family or friends move or sadly pass away. Suddenly, the idea of somewhere new—perhaps following family or friends— may be very appealing. Many have moved from north Jersey to south Jersey. And some have moved even farther south to the Carolinas or even "God's waiting room," otherwise known as

Florida. The lower cost of living, and homes in general, can be attractive.

These folks have "cashed in" and sold their house and moved and pocketed the difference for an enormous windfall. If they had a reverse mortgage, not only could they not have cashed in, but for some, they may not have been able to sell at all because they owed too much on their home.

The overriding theme here is that it is always good to have choices—especially down the road when you don't know what your circumstances will be. I tell my clients all the time, "Always keep your options open. Don't lock yourself in. You'll be glad later on." And they always are.

Having options and choices adds happiness to life.

CHAPTER 9

Money—And What It Represents

Growing up in Smalltown, USA (aka Point Pleasant Beach, New Jersey) in the 1970s and early '80s was really a great experience. Anyone can tell you that our shore community was very special for most of us. With the beach, boardwalk, and ocean within walking distance, it was always fun and exciting.

Most of the town was made up of middle-class families, many of whom moved there from North Jersey. I was one of these "bennies" as they were known. When I was five, my parents jumped on the chance to buy their first house on Cramer Ave near the Beach High School. I had to walk to the G. Harold Antrim Elementary School across town every day and got to go through the middle of downtown. It was alive with small shops, including a Five-and-Dime and Woolworths that had a soda fountain counter. I remember being conscious of the different businesses and the friendly people that owned them and worked there.

I learned at a very young age that people had very different attitudes and beliefs about money and what it represented. Here's what I saw and learned as a pre-teen living down the shore.

My mom became involved with our church—St Peter's—and helped start and run the group that gave all the senior citizens something to attend and look forward to each week. Because I was young (under ten), I got to go to some of their events and was able to "help out" as best I could. At these events, the church would provide free food, including desserts. Well, of course, everyone would not only eat their lunch, but they would also take "extras" to bring home. My Mom thought it was cute and always encouraged the seniors to take more. (As an aside, almost forty years later, I would have my own events, including Lunch & Learns, and would do the same thing for our clients and guests).

Most everyone took their fair share of extras, but this one couple Mr. and Mrs. F___ really loaded up their old station wagon with what looked to me to be a month's supply of sandwiches and desserts. I looked on in awe, and my mom would even see me with my mouth open, give me a look, and take me aside to explain to me that Mr. and Mrs. F___ were very poor and it was okay for them to take extra. I remember thinking, "They've got to be the poorest people in Point Pleasant Beach to be taking home that much free food!" Not only that, but they were also . . . how can I say this nicely . . . just nasty. They both had these attitudes that everyone owed them not just free food, but free labor, too. They had me and other kids come to their house to do yard work and other errands for them . . . and of course to help carry in all the boxes of free food they were taking. My young mind thought this was hysterical and rationalized that they were probably poor because of how they treated other people. But my mom and the church seemed to be bottomless in their generosity.

This went on for years until finally one day, they both died—not on the same day, but within a few months of each other. I remember thinking they will probably have to take a special offering to pay for their funeral. Sheesh was I wrong! The whole community was in shock when it was found out that not only were they not poor, but they had hundreds of thousands of dollars in CASH stuffed everywhere in their house! It was like the stories you hear of the homeless person with a shopping cart filled with money. All I could think about (in my young mind) was how do I put in a claim for the endless hours of free labor I gave to these people thinking they were too poor to rub two nickels together.

A different type of person I met was in the local sandwich shop only a few blocks from our house. Back in the '70s, I would walk or ride my bike to this shop maybe 2-3 times a week to get a sandwich or at least a bag of potato chips or a cookie. The owner was young and always there with a smile on his face when I walked in to get my 25-50 cents worth of food. He would go out of his way to make the goofy kid that I was feel welcome in his store . . . sometimes giving me free slices of meat or even a free bag of potato chips. When I didn't have enough for what I wanted, he'd just say "Ahh, you can pay me next time, Billy." But when next time came, he never took the money.

I saw that he was not just generous with me, but with everyone that walked in. It wasn't like he could afford to be so giving, but he just was. And you know what? People loved him for it. It was an interesting contrast to the people who had money stuffed everywhere in their house and were miserable and living with scarcity minds.

That young sandwich shop owner's name was Peter Cancro. He was the owner of Mike's Submarines, which became Jersey Mike's, and grew into one of the most successful franchises in the country. Mr. Cancro is known for his extreme generosity, having raised and given away millions of dollars to local and national charities and foundations. He is a local hero and celebrity and is revered in the Jersey shore business community.

What makes a person live a life that is so filled with kindness and giving, especially during times when they didn't have any extra means, and then continue to do so as their life and business grew and succeeded? And what makes others hoard every penny and live as if they were broke into their senior years, being mean and nasty to other people, all while having hundreds of thousands of dollars stuffed in their drawers and mattresses?

Each of us has our own personal psychology of money. Good or bad, it can evolve or change. The person who mentored me in the financial services industry and who's been my best friend for years is also one of the most generous and giving people I've ever met. Similar to Peter Cancro, Glenn Romer (another Point Pleasant Beach native) has given financial contributions to people and causes large and small. He keeps his philanthropy anonymous most of the time, but I've seen him go above and beyond to help anyone in need. Yet Glenn wasn't always like this. As the toughest kid in the mean streets of Point Pleasant Beach, he shook everyone down for quarters and sometimes dollars for video games at the boardwalk. We would all have to bring extra quarters with us for Glenn so we'd be able to play without getting punched in the arm until we surrendered our money. I also learned from Glenn's family that when he got home from school or work, he would go in the bathroom and wash all his coins and dollars . . . such was his love and obsession for money.

Over his young adult years, Glenn would transform himself from this angry small-town bully to the giving person that he is today. For him, it took close calls with his own mortality to awaken him spiritually and transform him into a contributing citizen of the human race.

Both of these Point Pleasant Beach natives enjoy giving back and making a difference. Their attitudes towards money can be a lesson for everyone, but especially those nearing retirement age here in New Jersey.

One time some years ago, I was driving up the Garden State Parkway coming home from Atlantic City. I liked to escape there with my friends now and then to play cards or just eat at their buffets. This was before EZ-Pass and before the toll booths were consolidated. The parkway had multiple tolls that cost an average of fifty cents each. We all remember there were token or exact change lanes that you could go through by tossing coins or tokens into a big basket that stuck out as you drove past. There were also the lanes where you gave a toll operator a dollar and they gave you change.

As I pulled up to a toll booth to give my dollar, it was an extra wide lane – and I was farther away from the toll booth than normal. The person in the booth looked miserable. I stretched my hand out far to try and reach the toll collector, but this person who was probably close to retirement age would not put her hand out beyond her toll booth.

I actually thought she was joking around and smiled at her and said, "Hey what's going on?" as I reached as far as I could over to her, extending the dollar bill in my hand.

She looked back at me in a sad, but also angry, manner.

"I never reach out to anyone. I stopped reaching out to people years ago," she replied.

I got out of my car to complete the transaction.

"Yeah, I can see that and how it's been so successful for you," I said before returning to my car and driving away.

Even though I never saw this person again, and I know nothing about her or her situation, she showed herself to be in a miserable state of existence. I always remember her line: "I stopped reaching out to people years ago."

It seems clear that when we stop reaching out and stop giving to others, we are actually going against the way we are supposed to be. This transcends our spiritual beliefs and our faith in God or lack thereof. If you really think about it, we are all at our best when we are giving of ourselves.

It doesn't have to just be money, but money is both the hardest and easiest thing to give away. It can be the hardest because it is tangible and represents a real value that we earned from our own labor, so mentally it can seem hard to give away actual cold hard cash. Yet it can also be the easiest because, unlike time, it can be replenished. When you give money to a cause or an individual in need, you're only giving something that while tangible, can be replaced with future income.

Maybe you've heard the saying, "The secret to living is giving." While it's simple and corny, for those who realize it, it's a game-changer in life and financial planning. By giving something away, it seems to create in our minds the idea that there is always abundance—always extra. The Peter Cancros and Glenn Romers know this. Peter seemed to know it from the start, while Glenn learned it at a young age.

Some go through their whole lives and sadly never realize this secret. Maybe they're not as bad as the couple I met who had hundreds of thousands of dollars in cash hidden all over their house while appearing to be destitute, but they're still not aware of the power of giving.

As part of your retirement plan, either on your own or with your advisor (if you're working with one), come up with a dollar figure from your retirement income that you will give away. Or better yet, consider just being on the lookout for areas where there is a need and just give. The feeling will be euphoric—especially if you do it anonymously so that you have nothing to gain. Regardless of how you do it, this attitude can be a game changer.

By giving away something, you'll start to treat yourself better, too! The change that can happen from scarcity to abundance will affect you not just financially but in your overall well-being.

When people across the country think of us from New Jersey, they often make the mistake of thinking we are selfish, obnoxious, and ignorant. But you and I know better. The families and individuals that I help and serve are the most wonderful, caring, and selfless citizens of the United States and the planet.

CHAPTER 10

FOMO

I f you're over fifty years old, you will naturally remember the time before the internet, before cell phones, and even before computers were readily available. Without texting, email, or actual calls on our cell phones, you only had a couple of ways for a friend to reach you quickly. This was either on your home phone, which was hard-wired in your house . . . or . . . and forgive me for how crazy this might seem . . . you actually had to listen for your doorbell or a knock on your front door! That's it. There was no other way for your friends or anyone else to reach you on short notice.

In Point Pleasant Beach, New Jersey, during the 1970s, my friends didn't call. They came over and knocked on the door or yelled through the screen door. "Come-on, Skillender! We've got Russell, Rhys, Billy Dwyer, Billy Stoughton, and Billy Johnson all set for the kickball game. Teddy Durante and Mike Mercuro are coming, too, so we just need you and we've got a full game." Anticipating their arrival, I had my old Kmart sneakers already on with my cut-off shorts, and I was ready to go. This was the best part of my day, and there was no way I would miss it. That's why I waited near my front door and listened for their arrival.

But imagine what would happen if I missed them stopping by? I just couldn't. I had to be there ready to play. I didn't realize it at the time, but I was being programmed (like almost everyone else) with what is now known as FOMO . . . Fear of Missing Out.

Today, this FOMO is prevalent everywhere. It can get in the way of a happy, fulfilling retirement. Think about it: You may not realize it, but it is ingrained in our thinking. I don't know for sure if it's because we developed it (like how I was afraid of missing a kickball game) or if it's actually in our DNA from the start. But we have to recognize it and understand it.

Of course, I thought it was just me that always was afraid of missing out on something, but once I became an advisor and began speaking to hundreds of individuals and families, I realized just how detrimental it is. "If these walls could speak ..." is something I always say when I'm told something to illustrate that so many others have similar stories.

And even though I'm making light of it by bringing up a childhood fear of missing the best kickball game on my side of the railroad tracks, this fear can be profoundly debilitating. We've all been through it with the pandemic. It seemed like our lives stopped or worse. Now we're overloaded with the thought of missing out on something. The idea that our time is really limited and we can't do what we thought we were going to do can put us in a painful state of mind.

In my early days with Lincoln Financial, there were clients who came to me and liked me, so they opened up an account. When I asked them if they had other advisors or accounts anywhere, they often listed over twenty financial institutions and advisors—everyone from the biggest wirehouses on down to an insurance salesman working out of the trunk of his car . . . and many people in between.

I asked them with genuine curiosity why they had so many advisors. You'll never guess what they said: "Because we don't want to miss out on anything." They went on to explain that they attended every seminar, workshop, and lecture that is available. Sometimes, it would be two a day, every day. They also listened to radio shows to get all the information they provided.

While I thought it was kind of quirky and weird to have so many different advisors and ideas coming at them from all different directions, I didn't know just how debilitating it could be until after they were put in a nursing home and had to help their family with the account they had with me.

Their children were exhausted in telling me that they had so many accounts spread out in so many places that all their different investments contradicted each other. It was like they diversified so much that it hurt them. When one account went up, another one went down.

Their FOMO also stopped them from enjoying life. They had such a full schedule of workshops that they did nothing else. They weren't coming for the free meals, just information, because most of the workshops only offered coffee at most. What a terrible way to spend one's golden years: listening to people like me drone on about finances and investments!

As you might suspect, FOMO is most prevalent in investing. I saw it and experienced it personally back when I was an options trader. Imagine being on a trading floor in the 1990s, and the whole room is celebrating their success by seemingly all making the right trade at the right time in the right stock or option. You'd feel pretty left out if you weren't in on it, as any of us did. Fast-forward to current times, and you've heard how everyone you know has supposedly made a fortune in cryptocurrency or something similar. Sound familiar? Again, how does it feel when you're not part of what it seems like everyone else is?

Remember the market in 2007 at its all-time high at the time? Remember your friends and neighbors bragging about their accounts? I remember thinking at the time—in my early forties—that I needed to be more aggressive or I was going to miss out on this bull market. Fortunately, I didn't think that way for my clients at the time and had them in conservative investments. For myself, however, I went all in—almost at the market peak—and then it tanked. I did not miss out, all right—on the market crash.

What can we do to stop ourselves from feeling like we're going to miss out, whether it be on the bull market run or on something else? How can we get ourselves not to look around at everything else? It may be impossible to fully change if FOMO really is built into our DNA, but maybe we can at least remember the idea that the present is the present. It's so simple, it's almost goofy. But think about it. There are all these sayings out there. Among them: "Live today because tomorrow is never promised."

When we truly realize that we have the present (and view it as a present), then everything changes. We may not lose our FOMO completely, but our perception of what really matters will override our FOMO mindsets.

The clients that are the happiest are not the wealthiest in terms of dollars. They are the ones who have been through life's good and bad like everyone else, but more than anything, they live in the present—whatever that means to them. This could be spending time with friends and loved ones, playing golf or cards, or volunteering their time and energy.

One of my favorite quotes is from Emerson: "The purpose of life is not to be happy. It is to be useful, to be honorable, to be compassionate, to have made some difference that you have lived and lived well."

Again, we may not fully cure FOMO, but if we remember this one simple idea, then I believe we will be fulfilled and, in turn, happy beyond our wildest dreams.

CHAPTER 11

When Disaster Hits...

This chapter could be a book unto itself, and I had initially thought about just waiting to actually write a whole new book on this topic. But I realized that this is too important to wait because almost everyone has at some time or another been punched in the gut by life . . .

A sudden loss—or even one that's not sudden—can wreak havoc on our well-being. Sadly, especially during COVID-19, we've had so many of our clients and client families lose their spouses or other close family members. Some have lost children or grandchildren. No one can know what it is like for that person to go through the unthinkable. A part of ourselves is no longer here, and we're left behind, forced to somehow continue on.

A divorce or separation can leave its own unique scars. And we can't dismiss the agonizing experience of having someone we love go through a slow mental and or physical decline.

Alongside all of the emotional and physical pain that these horrible situations cause, there's financial strain, too. You may wonder how you're going to make it through each day.

While I'm not in a position to give advice or counsel on getting through the grief, I would like to offer some thoughts that may point you in the right direction regarding finances.

First is to know that you may be in what, for lack of a better term, is a "fog." I've seen and experienced my own losses in my life, and there's a type of post-traumatic stress that we as human beings are susceptible to. We are therefore in a vulnerable position.

It is important to "circle the wagons," so to speak. That means you want to find those whom you are close to and trust fully. That is most often a family member, but it could be a lifelong friend, too. You want this person or persons to be your "anchor." When you're going through this storm, your anchor is there holding you secure.

With this person there with you, they can be your eyes and ears while you're in the "fog" and getting your financial house in order. You'll want them to be your sounding board, too. You may have plans that need to be reviewed and reconsidered.

The next step is to (as best as you can) get all your financial information into one place. Take an inventory of everything. Simply use a blank piece of paper to write down all your assets. On another page, write down all your liabilities. Finally, on another page, list all your monthly income and monthly expenses.

Now that you have all of this in as simple a form as possible, you'll want to find a professional to help. There are many financial advisors out there, as I've gone over in a previous chapter. Most are competent, and many are fiduciaries, meaning they are required to act in their client's best interests. But especially now, you want someone that you are also comfortable with, and that you feel good talking with and listening to. This may or may not be the financial advisor you or your family were currently using. That is also why having that trusted friend or family member with you as your eyes and ears is important. They can most likely make a better judgment on someone or reinforce your own judgment during this stressful time.

Most importantly, you want someone who will not add to your stress. At least in this one area of your life, they can take some stress away. I would think it would be someone that you see yourself being able to speak freely with both now and in the years ahead.

Finances are one part of your life, but don't be afraid to reach out for help in other areas as well. Mental, physical, and spiritual well-being are also important, and help is available.

CHAPTER 12

How Bad Is It Going to Get?

All of us (advisors and individual investors) are geniuses when the market is going up. We feel validated that we did our research or due diligence and after careful analysis made our proper allocations, and everything worked out beautifully. I've mentioned when I was trading options in the 1990s with such massive success and thinking, "Why didn't I start doing this when I was eighteen?"

When the tech bubble burst in 2000, I realized that I was actually not the New Jersey version of Warren Buffet. Even worse, nothing I did with trading seemed to work.

But I was in my late twenties to early thirties during that period, so, fortunately, while very painful, I could actually recover and even learn from my early failures as a trader. But what happens if you're close to retirement or even in retirement and you're dealing with investments that have been going down almost every day for most of the year (which is exactly what's happening in the market as I write this in July 2022)?

Let's look at the good and the bad of the stock market declines.

First, the bad: over the past 130-plus years of market history, the obvious worst time was The Great Depression, which started with the market crash of 1929. Most people are shocked when I ask them to imagine that they had their money in the stock market in October 1929 and it crashed, and then guess how long it took for the market to come back and their investments to recover. If you had $100,000 or $1 million, how long would it be not to even grow above that number but just to get back to even? Most guess five years, or then realize the Depression lasted throughout the 1930s, so they guess ten years. When I tell them that it was actually twenty-five years—1954, to be exact—that it took an investment to be back to even, almost everyone is astonished. To have to go through all that time: The Depression, World War II, and finally almost halfway into the 1950s. The idea of their investments going down and possibly never coming back in their lifetime is terrifying.

While this is horrible, I then remind them that in more recent history, the market downturns do not last anywhere near twenty-five years. We had the "lost decade," of course, which was the start of the 21st century, but since The Great Recession of 2008, there are more safeguards in place to maybe not fully prevent a market downturn, but to help offset a complete collapse.

Now the good news: the more recent downturns lasted months or possibly a couple of years, not decades. With all this in mind, the question remains. What do you do when your investments are going down? Well, the answer is . . . it depends . . .

Now hang in there with me. I'm not just trying to give you a cute answer here, especially for something so important. Let me explain what I mean.

It depends on where you are in life. If you are five to ten years from retirement, then you can take advantage of this market downturn and using dollar-cost averaging, actually add to your good investments. When I say "good" investments, I mean things that have a track record like large-cap stocks held in the S&P 500 Index, not fly-by-night penny stocks or other speculative plays. But by dollar-cost averaging into your investments, over time, you will more than likely come out okay.

If, however, you are one or two years from retirement or even actually in retirement and your account is going down, and you are or will be shortly taking funds out of your account to support your retirement, then you will need to make some adjustments.

The right advisor helping you is like having the right doctor when you are sick. Just like a person with injuries, you have to stop the bleeding first. Taking money out of an account that is going down causes what I call "reverse dollar-cost averaging," which is possibly dangerous and harmful to your retirement account's health (and in turn your own health and well-being).

The amount that should be at risk in the market when you're taking funds out should arguably be much lower than the old rule of thumb: take your age and subtract it from one hundred and that is the percentage you should have at risk. But then, would you really want to be sixty-five or seventy years old and have 30-35 percent of your account going down as you are withdrawing?

Again, I can't say this enough: this is especially the time when professional guidance is imperative. The situation requires a financial advisor working under the fiduciary standard, who would do everything in your best interest to navigate you through this very dangerous situation.

We know that the right doctor or surgeon can be the difference between life and death. Besides their actual knowledge and skills, if you're their patient, then you KNOW they are doing everything possible, and you have confidence in them and their guidance. That confidence can sometimes be the difference in how things turn out. You wouldn't want to be going it alone with a major health concern for yourself or your loved ones. It's like having the weight of what you're dealing with almost lifted off of you with the right professional on your side.

While your physical health is more important than anything, your financial health has its own priority. And the right answers to the "what to do?" questions can make all the difference in the real world and also inside our heads, giving us peace of mind. So many of my clients and families just want to know that they're okay or that they're going to be okay . . . and when I'm able to tell them that yes, you're okay, it's one of the most rewarding things about my job . . . like a doctor giving their patient a clean bill of health and the patient is relieved and grateful for the good news.

CHAPTER 13

Do I Really Need a Financial Advisor?

hen people make their initial visit to my office, one of the first questions I typically hear is, "Why do I need an advisor? After all, I've done this well myself; what can you or any other advisor possibly do for me?"

They may be right: Perhaps an advisor isn't needed, especially when there is more access to information than ever before. At the end of 2021, the market had continued to reach all-time highs, and there seemed to be no signs of slowing down. We know that in the long run, the market always goes up. So why not just use the market to invest in a simple S&P mutual fund or ETF and let the gains and dividends provide us with what is needed for retirement?

I understand how people would want to do this themselves or have a trusted family member with some experience in the stock market help them. The financial services industry has gained such a bad reputation over the years, whether it was from movies like

"Wolf of Wall Street" or from the Bernie Madoffs that have further eroded confidence in true financial planners.

You may recall I used the term "fiduciary" earlier. These days, that term is thrown around a lot. It's not a new word by any means. It comes from the Latin word Fidere which means "to trust." And more recently it was mentioned in a court ruling from 1830, which states "a prudent person standard of care." In the simplest terms, it just means having the client's best interest first, before anything else.

A few years ago, the financial industry came out with the Certified Financial Fiduciary designation. It required a clean history with clients, i.e., no complaints for ten years. It also required an extensive study course and exam. I achieved this designation thinking that it would help solidify my credentials with my clients and prospective clients. Even with this designation, however, does that give me or anyone else the presumptive advantage to work with you?

I like to think of my own experiences with "advisors" from different fields to help answer the question: Over the course of my own life, both personally and professionally, I was fortunate in that I never really had any legal issues and therefore had no need for a lawyer.

I am learning a similar lesson when it comes to doctors. Again, for my whole adult life, I have been very fortunate not having any serious health issues. But now, having just turned fifty-five, I've come to realize that the right doctor can be extremely helpful in preventing illness and offering peace of mind knowing that I'm under the best care. That's an incredible feeling.

Which brings me back to financial advisors: What can they really offer? Let me just say that most financial advisors really want to do what's right for their clients. Most do have their client's best interests in mind in everything that they do. There are really only a few Madoffs out there that give a bad name to the entire industry.

Allow me to take it one step further, however. Just because someone has one's best interest in mind doesn't mean that they are truly capable of doing what's best for the client—even though they want to with all their heart.

It takes a certain knowledge and specialty in retirement planning to be able to do the absolute best for you. Let me go back to my attorney analogy: when I was involved in a legal dispute (and to be clear, this had nothing to do with my financial advice), I was referred to an attorney who specialized in exactly the type of law in which I needed help. There are thousands of attorneys in New Jersey, most of whom are reputable and would have my best interest at heart. But there are only a few that specialize in the type of law that I needed help with, and I found what I learned was one of the best, if not THE best, to handle my situation and get me through with a positive result.

I jokingly say sometimes that there are also thousands of financial advisors licensed in New Jersey and many more unlicensed who think they are financial advisors. Most of them also probably would have the best interest of their clients in everything they do. But there is only a small amount that practice true retirement income planning. We focus on this and therefore have an acute knowledge of this type of investing and planning. We are also aware of things here in New Jersey that may be specific to our demographics. As with both the specialist attorney and doctor, the guidance is actually valuable before there is a major problem, not just after it happens.

The market can sometimes look like it's never going to go down. I remember the same feelings of the market euphoria in the 1990s when I was trading options. All I had to do was buy and hold. If the position went down, as long as I held a day or week or maybe a month longest, it always recovered and went up. I couldn't lose. I was too smart for my own good, but then when the market did go down . . . and stay down for most of the next decade (hence the term "lost decade"), then I learned that I wasn't that smart and had a lot to learn.

So it is with our physical health and financial health: when everything is going well, there is no perceived need for any help. But the right advisor can and will be there while things are good and make sure you're okay if things take a bad turn.

Imagine your comfort knowing that someone has your back. I have clients that love to get into the intricate details of their investments and accounts, and they want to know how they work in good and bad markets. I have other clients that just want a "big picture" overview of their accounts and don't want to get bogged down in the details. I have still others that are in between these two extremes. There is no right or wrong. I simply adjust to each person or family and help them know beyond a doubt that this is one area of their life that they do not have to stress over. These days, there's enough stress out there, and alleviating this one part can make an enormous difference.

To recap: Why do you need a financial advisor? Or a doctor? Or an attorney? Even if you would rather do everything yourself when it comes to finances or your health, or your legal exposure, maybe at the very least consider the good it might do for your loved ones to have the right people available and able to provide answers and guidance to them.

Finally, as you search for the right advisor, I believe when you find the right one, you'll know it—especially if you have a close friend or family member referring you to them. As part of what I do for my clients, I offer myself as a sounding board for their people at no cost to be available to answer any questions. Many times, it may be an area of financial services in which I do not focus. In such instances, I tell them right away and try to point them in the right direction. For others, I can be truly helpful, and even if they don't become my client, I can at least give some input to help them get clarity on what they should be doing.

CHAPTER **14**

Who's a Good Fit?

Once you conclude that you'd like to work with a financial advisor and would feel better having someone be that "second pair of eyes" for you, the obvious question is who might be a good fit.

What questions should I ask the advisor and/or myself? Upon what should I focus? What red flags do people commonly miss because they don't know to watch for them? Are there GREEN flags we should watch for as well?

I believe that a prospective advisor who has no complaints against them is important and should be one of the first things to look for. But there are some other things that run deeper. I always think, "What would I be looking for if it was me?" Or even better, "Whom should it be if my parents were still alive and needed to find the right advisor?"

One of the best places to start is with a prospective advisor's current clients—especially if you know them personally. A current client, especially a long-term one, can give you insights that can go beyond whether they have a certain designation or even have no complaints against them.

Asking questions such as, "How do they treat you?" or, "How do they make you feel?" can be a start that will give you some deeper answers. "Do you feel confident with their advice? Or does what they are doing for you make you toss and turn at night?"

This is the best way to possibly narrow down whom you would consider, but there is nothing better than spending about an hour in a face-to-face meeting. I believe that you'll get a real feel for the person that goes beyond designations and a clean record. You don't have to have them be your best friend, but I think just asking the question, "Do I like this person as a human being?" can be very helpful.

No offense to the new crop of young, energetic advisors, but I think that an advisor who has had life experiences can be helpful. For example, someone can read about the 1929 market crash and ensuing Depression, but unless you lived through it, you just cannot understand the pain and despair. It's the same way with the 2008 market crash, which began the Great Recession. No one can imagine what it was like (unless you were at this point in your life) to have just retired in 2008 and then see your portfolio cut in half . . . or worse. Just imagine having to go back to work at some menial job just to get by! I remember families coming into my office from seminars and workshops, and their faces showed their complete devastation because they had worked their whole lives to get to this point, and almost instantly, they were wiped out. Their pain was so real that it was palpable.

Living through this gives a unique perspective and healthy respect for the market and investing. And on the other hand, so did living through the '90s market seemingly going straight up: being blindfolded and throwing a dart at the board, and everything working out well because the market was in an uptrend until the tech bubble burst in 2000. The next few years were all down. To have been an options trader during this period again gave me a perspective and experience that I've found very helpful.

Now, I'm not saying that everyone who is young or who wasn't an options trader in the 1990s wouldn't be a great financial advisor; but living through something is much different than just reading about it. Remember in the movie Good Will Hunting, Robin Williams' character tried to explain to Matt Damon that he could only get so much out of reading about places or things. Unless you have experienced it, you just don't really know what it's like.

Your prospective advisor doesn't necessarily have to be your best friend, but the person should be someone that you would feel good about spending time with—especially since the time would be spent going over something as important as your retirement investments. Many advisors seem to think very highly of themselves, and it is important that they have confidence in what they do. But I've heard stories of advisors speaking to their clients in a condescending manner. They seem to do this to either intimidate their client or possibly to impress themselves. In my opinion, this type of behavior is not someone that would be helpful to you. That doesn't mean you have to find the nicest, most docile person in the world. Rather, look for someone who displays kindness and empathy as their overall personality traits. They can be very helpful especially during hard times.

Another possible sign of the right advisor is who they have on their team—or even if they have a team. There are many advisors who are one-person shops. While there may be nothing wrong with someone who does everything themselves, ask yourself: "Is this the person I want handling my retirement?" It's like going to your doctor, and he's the only one in the office. He explains, "Yeah, I do everything myself. This way, I can put all my attention on you." Would that make you feel good about your doctor? He is the receptionist, answers the phone, and does your bloodwork and other tests. Then if you need something serious done, he says to you, "Okay, can you help me while I put this bandage on you?" I think you get my meaning.

Something else to consider is the advisor's office . . . or maybe lack of office? There may be some very competent, diligent advisors working out of a subpar office or even out of their car in some cases, but just like your doctor: Is their office situation one that makes you feel comfortable? I try to think about it as if the situation was reversed or if my parents were still alive. I don't mean to judge the person, but this is your retirement we're talking about. As I've said before, there is no "do-over" or "reset" button if you get it wrong.

Whether or not the prospective advisor is part of a big firm or independent also is important. The big firms may seem to have more resources, but this can be deceptive. I started at a big firm.

Lincoln Financial had been around for over one hundred years, it had a great reputation, and so on. But what I learned was big firms want their advisors to use their investments. LFG has a lot of good choices that they wanted us to use instead of everything else available. I realized this limited me to what I could offer my clients. When I went independent, I was able to use not just what Lincoln had to offer, but everything else out there.

I realize that for some, the security of a big firm may be important. But if you can get past this idea, then the independent advisor's ability to have access to every investment available is something to seriously consider.

CHAPTER 15

The World Really Can Be Your Oyster

Once you have a plan in place—one you've put together on your own or with your advisor—and you know what your income will be from all sources (including dividends and interest, Social Security, pensions, and other government benefits), you will know what you can spend and what you can do.

There's an old saying that goes along the lines of, "Don't make things better than they are, but don't make them worse than they are." In other words, this is where you are and now you go from there. You have your income and expenses and know what you can now do with your life.

Here's the really good news: here in New Jersey, the world really is your oyster. To start with, the free or virtually free things that we have right here down the shore: There are beautiful beaches and boardwalks that can offer solitude or crowds or anything in between. I live in Toms River, but I still love my hometown of Point Pleasant Beach. The boardwalk on spring or autumn nights offers what I feel is the real juice of life—the ocean and sand. Downtown offers easy streets to walk along, and if you get hungry, one of my best friends has a famous pizza place called Rosie's that has won every award for pizza in and around New Jersey.

Within a short drive are historic landmarks such as Allaire State Park, offering peaceful trails and retail shops. Farther down the parkway is Popcorn Park Zoo, which I think is very therapeutic and relaxing. Then there's the public library system in Monmouth and Ocean Counties. All of these free books and resources are available to all residents.

Most of these amenities cost nothing or close to nothing. (Well, maybe not Rosie's Pizza—Mike gets over $20 a pie, but it is worth it. ☺) But seriously, all these things we take for granted are right outside our door. It's truly unreal when you realize what we have access to in our little community here and what it means to be able to just look at the beach or ocean and enjoy the salt air.

After enjoying things that are free or almost free, then there are things that cost just a little. There are so many things here in New Jersey that are really inexpensive; I myself forget sometimes. There are shows and events all around us. For example: in Red Bank is the Count Basie Theater. Over the years, I've seen some incredible concerts and events there, including the bands Toto and America. These are small, intimate concerts that cost $49-89 a seat. We've actually taken our whole team to the Basie to see Frankie Valley and had dinner next door at Buona Sera. Then we

NEW JERSEY RETIREMENT ROADMAP • 97

all stayed overnight at the Molly Pitcher Inn. It was such a great time, but I'm not trying to brag about taking our team out. I just want to say that for a reasonable price, you can make a day and night out of it.

There are other things that aren't too pricey all around us. In Atlantic City at the Borgata and some of the other casinos, they have comedy shows that are usually either free (with a casino card) or cost $20. These shows are fun, and while I'm not really a gambler (except for an occasional poker game), there are great restaurants and overnight accommodations at each casino.

Getting a little more expensive, but still reasonable, are the trains, buses, and boat rides that can take us to all that is available in and around New Jersey. A little over an hour by train is New York City or Philadelphia. A little farther is Washington, D.C., or Connecticut. Then there are the SeaStreak boats that go to New York. These are all not free, but very reasonably priced. Most of the events, such as Broadway shows, and so many other cultural things, can also be done without spending an arm and a leg.

The Jersey Shore really can provide endless options that can be rewarding to us, especially after the pandemic we've all been through. Besides doing things and having experiences, I believe that our lives should be about more. Most everyone has experienced loss; some unbearable. Going through life and losing people you love has an effect that no one else can understand. Even if they've been through it themselves, they cannot know exactly what you've been through.

When I was younger and experienced losing my mom and other family and friends that I loved and could not fathom my life without, I searched for someone who had experienced loss. I tried to find what it was that brought them out of the abyss.

I discovered Robert Kennedy, who had actually died only a year after I was born. He changed his life after his brother JFK was killed and basically became an entirely different person who threw himself into changing the very fabric of life in the world. He lived by and often quoted Ralph Waldo Emerson's idea that "The purpose of life is not to be happy. It is to be useful, to be honorable, to be compassionate, to have it make some difference that you have lived and lived well."

I think that if we actually do what Emerson says, it will result in happiness. There is nothing more fulfilling than making a difference in the lives around us. For me, I can never bring back any of my people who have left this world. But, through doing what I do every day, I can bring them alive in my words and actions. By no means am I trying to preach or provide proper grief counseling. But I do believe that through our grief, we can find something more than ourselves and be a tiny ripple of hope to ourselves and those around us.

This all comes back to the idea that money should be used as a tool and not a hindrance. Whatever the income is that you worked out by yourself or with your advisor, that is what you have to work with. But it does not define you or your life going forward. You need hardly any money or income to make a difference in a life, whether it's a friend, family, or stranger. You can use your time and life experience to do something significant and incredible, even if it's only for your child or grandchild.

That is when we know we are really rich: when we are using all of our talents to the absolute best of our abilities. The clients that I have that have discovered this "secret" are never bored or depressed. They wake up every day measuring themselves as to what they've done the day before. They realize that life is short, time is precious, and they want to impact other lives. In turn, they recognize they are wealthy beyond measure.

CHAPTER 16

For Younger Investors

Most of the individuals and families that I work with and help are at or near retirement age. I do have a few people that are in their forties and early fifties and still have a few years until retirement. But upon writing this book, it was brought to my attention that there are younger clients who also need guidance and direction. Given the recent volatility of the markets and the uncertainty about life after the COVID-19 pandemic, it's understandable.

Over the years, I've given out a copy of the classic book The Wealthy Barber by David Chilton. In this book (which is a great read for anyone, by the way), the story of saving and paying yourself first is told through a parable by a barber.

It reminds me of the clients of mine who told me their story of saving and amassing several million dollars over the course of their lives, all while both working regular jobs at their local supermarket making no more than $40,000 a year each.

How was this possible on their capped salaries? Simple: By using the power of dollar-cost averaging and the magic of compounding over time, their small but consistent contributions to their retirement accounts created an enormous nest egg. When you add in the power of dividends and reinvesting these as well, the potential is enormous.

What does this mean for someone younger right now, who has the power of time on their side, but not a lot to be able to contribute?

Someone who starts putting away $100 a week at the age of twenty-two and continues doing that until they reach age sixty-two, by compounding at 7 percent interest, would have over $1 million in their account! If the return is 9 percent (which is around the stock market average over the last 100-plus years)[6,] then they would have over $1.7 million.

Even though those numbers won't have the same buying power they do today, it still shows the effect that small, consistent saving and investing can have for someone young.

So exactly what should a young adult do about saving for retirement? Here are the steps that I recommend:

1. Work with an advisor. This is just as important for someone young because the right advisor will get them on the right track sooner than later.

---

[6] James Royal, PH.D., Arielle O'Shea. NerdWallet. December 8, 2022. "What Is the Average Stock Market Return?" https://www.nerdwallet.com/article/investing/average-stock-market-return

2. Make sure you use the right accounts and know the tax implications. Again, the right advisor will know this and guide you properly by hopefully taking full advantage of Roth IRAs and other tax-efficient options that are possible.

3. Read The Wealthy Barber book. Even with the right advisor, this can be so helpful and almost provide further evidence of the power of saving and investing consistently more than just speaking with your advisor. It will reinforce that you are being given good advice.

The power of time and especially taking advantage and utilizing tax-efficient strategies can't be emphasized enough. You may also need to speak with a CPA that is proactive, not just reactive. By that, I mean most accountants will do taxes and tell you what you owe or get back at tax time. The ones who are proactive will help you strategize and figure things out BEFORE tax time.

If you can find a financial advisor who has access to a proactive CPA or accountant, then you're way ahead of the game. I see it so often, and it's common in many of us: investors try and "chase yield" and go after and usually get that extra 1-2 percent. But in doing so, they ignore the tax implications, which can sometimes cost tens or even hundreds of thousands of dollars in extra taxes. These are real dollars that could have been in the investor's pocket instead of in the hands of the IRS.

Finally, the idea of saving for retirement should not be something painful that would dampen your life. Treat it like just another monthly expense, like a utility bill, car payment, or insurance payment that you do automatically. It may mean making some sacrifices for a while, but the rewards will be well worth it in the long run.

CHAPTER 17

A Final Message

I f there is one thing I hope you get from reading this book, it's the lesson I've gleaned from thousands of hours of meetings with hundreds of New Jersey families and individuals: The secret to a happy retirement is not about assets. It's about risk management and lifetime income.

My happiest clients are the ones who take income from their accounts on a monthly basis. Their retirement income has replaced their employment income. My unhappiest clients were the ones who just wanted their assets to grow. Do you remember the couple who lived in the trailer park off Route 70 who appeared to not have two nickels (or even two pennies) to rub together? In reality, they had over $6 million in investments—and they were miserable. Even my theory of them getting fulfillment from watching their account go up every year wasn't enough to make them happy.

When they became my clients, I was only able to help them with the risk management part of their portfolio. I moved them into conservative investments just before the financial crisis of 2008, which would have provided them with substantial income. But you know the story . . . they chose to just reinvest their income and deprive themselves of not just enjoying their golden years, but also of being able to help their children and grandchildren while they could.

I have used them (anonymously, of course) as a kind of warning to many of my clients. I hope it comes through here too: whether you work with a financial advisor or do it all yourself, make sure you take monthly income.

I think for every reason, it's best to work with a professional, someone who would have your best interests in mind and who is also competent. Someone recently told me that they feel like having an advisor is like having the right dentist. He said he wouldn't want to buy a drill and set up a chair in his garage and try to do that himself, either. While I would hope that what I do is not as painful as pulling teeth—and if you find yourself reacting that way with your advisor, I strongly suggest looking for another one—I understood the idea he was trying to convey.

I believe that most advisors are good people who really do put their client's interests first. There is only a small group of Bernie Madoffs out there looking to purposely hurt their unsuspecting clients.

But there are quite a few advisors who present themselves as professionals, yet don't have the competence and experience to do what is needed to create income and manage risk. If you're in doubt as to whom to work with, it's wise to be patient and keep

NEW JERSEY RETIREMENT ROADMAP • 107

looking until you find someone you're comfortable with. You don't want to put yourself in the wrong hands. You may be better off not having anyone help you than having an incompetent advisor handling your investment portfolio.

Now that you've read this book, I hope you see the importance of having a plan, and how a financial professional can help you reach your goals in retirement. I welcome the opportunity to meet with anyone, no matter their income level, to discuss how we may be able to help you achieve your unique milestones on the road to retirement.

Bill Skillender, Founder

As founder and senior wealth manager of William Skillender Wealth Management Tax Advisory, Bill is in the unique position of collaborating with leading experts on financial performance and achievement, as well as many of today's most successful investors, to uncover and share the secrets behind their extraordinary success.

Bill has nearly 20 years' experience in the financial services industry. Formerly a trader for a private firm in Philadelphia, Bill has always been interested in the stock market and investing. His business philosophy is to provide every person he meets with something beyond what they can get anywhere else. He gives each client customized, world-class service and attention so they can feel confident and empowered in the financial facet of their lives.

While many wealth managers have the drive to succeed, they lack the wisdom to harness their energy to benefit others. Bill and his team are dedicated to enhancing the quality of his clients' lives by helping them to create financial peace of mind through custom solutions to meet their individual needs, regardless of economic conditions.

Made in the USA
Middletown, DE
13 August 2024

58724975R00070